~~HAVE MO~~

~~RES~~

~~FROM CO~~

~~MENT~~

~~WILL~~

~~DON'T~~

~~OFF HER CHOMP~~

IT'S NOT MY FAULT THEY PRINT THEM

~~THE LOVE CHILD OF GERMAINE GREER & CHOPPER READ~~

~~PERFORMING MONKEY~~

~~IT WAS CRAP THE FIRST TIME~~

~~SHE'S ASKING FOR IT~~

~~JUST SHOOT HER~~

~~BETTER THE DEVENY YOU KNOW~~

~~GO IN SWINGING~~

~~DON'T GET ME STARTED~~

~~ACT YOUR AGE COLUMN~~

~~IS SHE FOR REAL?~~

~~HAVE TITS WILL TALK~~

~~LIFE LESSONS FROM A MAD WOMAN~~

~~SHE'S ASKING FOR IT~~

~~NO FEAR ... WELL, MAYBE A LITTLE~~

~~HASN'T SOMEONE KILLED HER YET?~~

~~BARKING MAD AND FULL OF SHIT~~

~~RAMBLINGS OF A DYSLEXIC FEMO-ATHEIST~~

~~UNINFORMED, ILL-ADVISED & OVER-RATED~~

~~BIGMOUTH STRIKES AGAIN~~

~~SHE BANGS~~

~~THIS WOMAN NEEDS A SLAP~~

~~BIG MOUTH. BAD TEETH~~

~~MOLE WITH A VIEW~~

IT'S NOT MY FAULT THEY PRINT THEM

*

Catherine
DEVENY

Black Inc.

Published by Black Inc.,
an imprint of Schwartz Publishing Pty Ltd
Level 5, 289 Flinders Lane
Melbourne Victoria 3000 Australia
email: enquiries@blackincbooks.com
http://www.blackincbooks.com

The National Library of Australia Cataloguing-in-Publication entry:

Deveny, Catherine, 1968- .
It's not my fault they print them.

1st ed.
ISBN 9781863951197 (pbk.).

1. Australia - Social life and customs - Anecdotes.
I. Title.

919.4

Book design by Thomas Deverall
Printed in Australia by Griffin Press

Contents

* Talking points *

* Australian comedy *

* Politics *

* The wide, wide world of TV *

For Marzy.
Who has cheered me on every step of the way,
despite numerous requests to "shut your wife up."

*

With thanks to the people who believed in me.
Especially: Sally Heath, Jonathan Green,
Suzanne Carbone, Louise Fox, Caitlin Crowley,
Michael Veitch, Guy Rundle, Rove McManus,
Marie-Louise Walker, Pat Deveny, Chris Feik,
Andrew Jaspan

*

Q&A with Catherine Deveny

My earliest memory is …
Going to a little boy's fifth birthday party, handing him a wrapped up matchbox car and saying "There you go Mark, it's lipstick."

At school I …
Was the dag with the buckteeth and the bad clothes.

I don't like talking about …
My sex change.

I wish I'd never worn …
A flannelette shirt and moccasins.

My mother always told me …
I was too loud. And if people asked, to tell them that she was my aunty.

I wish I had …
Become an atheist earlier.

I wish I hadn't …
Said cunt when I was hosting a ball for my kid's school.

It's not fashionable, but I love …
Barry Jones. And rissoles.

I'm very bad at …
Eating and not getting it on my clothes.

The book that changed my life is …
The Benny Hill Story.

Friends say I am …
A pain in the arse.

The song I'd like played at my funeral is …
"She Bangs".

The hardest thing I've ever done was …
Get over Keating losing the 1996 election.

What I don't find amusing is …
That funny smell in my fridge.

If I wasn't me I'd like to be …
One of my kids.

At the moment I'm reading …
Viz.

My favourite work of art is …
Still Life by Mario Strano.

I'm always being asked …
Do they pay you to write that stuff?

I often wonder …
How much I would get for my kids if I sold them for experiments.

Tell us something about the place where you grew up …
Reservoir. The only place in the world where people get married wearing tracksuits and where they have bouncers in the supermarkets.

Who would you like to be stuck next to on a long-haul flight?
Noam Chomsky. Or Louise Fox. Or Bill Hicks.

If you could be a character in a movie, who would you be?
Larry David from *Curb Your Enthusiasm.*

When was the last time you apologised?
Today. I drive an old Volvo with a SORRY sticker on the back window. It's not about the stolen generation, it's about my driving. And the environmental vandalism caused by driving such a wheezing old tractor.

What do you owe your parents?
Nothing.

What keeps you awake at night?
Sex.

What makes you happy?
Swearing.

Can you keep a secret?
Yes. But you have to tell me it's a secret, otherwise it ends up in one of my columns.

What was your favourite toy when you were little?
A doll called Gracie.

What happened to it?
My sons have poked her eyes out, chopped her hair off with a whipper snipper, given her a swallow tattoo on her neck, written on the back with texta "For a good time call Mum" and decapitated her.

If you had a spare $50, what would you spend it on?
The Asylum Seekers' Resource Centre. Or mullet haircuts for my sons.

What are you working on now?
Teaching my dyslexic son how to read (I'm dyslexic too). I saw this T-shirt the other day and it said DYSLEXICS UNTIE! Took me ages to get it. Seriously.

What is your favourite book?
The Dog Delusion by Richard Dawkins.

Do you imagine tomorrow will be better than today?
No.

What trait do you deplore in others?
Voting Liberal.

If you look out the window right now, what can you see?
Three nude dwarves punching each other up on the trampoline. Wait a second, that's my kids.

Sex, love & feminism

*

Surnames I

Who the hell is Jana Rawlinson? Jana Wendt I know, Jana Pittman I know, but Jana Rawlinson? So I check out the snap. It looks exactly like Jana Pittman. But her name is Jana Rawlinson. How bizarre. That has to be some crazy coincidence. A woman called Jana with a different surname who looks exactly like Jana Pittman. And, get this, she's a hurdler too. Freaky.

Oh, I get it. She has put a few noses out of joint in the past so she's keen on a bit of incognito action. You'd think she'd change her first name too. Then it dawned on me. She has got married, bizarre enough in itself these days, and changed her last name to her husband's. What an anachronism. Maybe she changed her name to go with the chastity belt, the crinolines and the stick "no thicker than his thumb" that her husband is allowed to beat her with.

Wake up! We are in 2007. Women are no longer owned by their father and then their husband. So why are some women still changing their surnames? And why do some men still want them to? It's sad, it's misogynous, it's archaic, it's insecure and it's unnecessary.

Why would you do something so drastic simply because you decided to delude yourself that it was easier? Because you are deeply insecure, deeply conservative or deeply stupid. And in deep denial.

I ask women why they changed their last name. They tell me "it's just easier." It's not. How easy is it to change the name on everything from your driver's licence to your library card? It's not. Many of the families I know have up to three different surnames and have no problem at all.

If people really believe that mum, dad and the kids

having the same surname is easier, why doesn't the guy change his name? Why don't they flip a coin and it's heads we go for her surname and tails we go for his? Because it is not about it being easier. It makes me despair. We've come all this way and we're still here.

Many women will say that their husbands wanted them to change their surname. So they did. Here's a flash for you, sister: if you do everything that your husband wants you to do, you may find yourself teetering round in a pair of stilettos and an apron all day saying, "Shall I fix some more food for you and the boys?" Or wearing a burqa.

Thanks to feminism, women should be allowed and encouraged to do anything they want. But the question I ask is: why do some women still want to change their surnames?

And not the stock answer they give, but why, deep in their hearts, they feel the need to dilute themselves.

So I kept reading the article and Jana has won a couple of gold medals. Good on her. She has an eight-month-old son and she was doing it for him. Here's a reality pill for you, Jana. You weren't doing it for him, you were doing it for you. He doesn't care.

Then it goes on to use the word "supermum" to describe her. How can a woman who has handed over her kid to be cared for by someone else while she has pursued her dreams with little or no thought to what the child needs or wants be described as a supermum? A supermum is a woman who has done the weekly shop with four kids under five and not killed any of them. If Jana had won the race with the baby strapped to her back while pushing a shopping trolley, I would have called her a supermum.

People are bagging Jana for putting her career above the

needs of her young child. Which I can understand. What I can't understand is why the father is not mentioned at all. And never is.

Whenever two parents are working and the child is propped up on the sideline waiting for its turn, why is it only the woman who gets bagged, as if the father has no responsibility for the care of his own child? Why, when a woman is working, does she always get asked, "Who's looking after your children?", but the father never does? We need to take the focus off the role of mother and put it onto parents as a team.

Men have become much more hands-on fathers in the past ten years and it has been magnificent to see. The kids, the dads and the mums have benefited greatly but we still have a long way to go. Dads, here's a sure-fire way of getting lucky tonight. Try this line: "I've made the lunches, done the reading and filled in all the excursion forms. The clothes are all laid out and I'm just going to put the kids to bed."

Surnames II

It looks like I've finally achieved my aim of whittling my readership down to three. So hello to Nana, Mum and Germaine – if you're still reading. Last week I wrote a column questioning, among other things, women taking their husband's surname. Talk about touchy! There were more noses out of joint than in a Jeff Fenech lookalike competition.

The response was massive, totally unexpected and absolutely fascinating. Reader feedback, the letters editor and the opinion editor were flabbergasted by the sheer volume of people wanting to put in their two cents. Even Kerri-Anne Kennerley bagged me. She was "offended," called me a "judgemental feminist" and said that I "probably couldn't get a man." I laughed for an hour. It seems you're either with me, or with Kerri-Anne ...

It was a case of Team Deveny versus Team How Dare You. Game on! Poke that animal in the cage!

I was shocked by what a deeply and blindly patriarchal society we still live in. How can this name thing still be an issue? Didn't they discuss this on the *Age*'s weekly women's-issues page, "Accent," in the 1970s?

I've poked the cages of private schools, clipboard-carrying parents, unnecessary caesareans, four-wheel drive owners, even God, and I have never been so overwhelmed by the response (equally positive and negative). Team How Dare You were extremely defensive and highly emotional. There was a stunning lack of clear rational thinking in every response. It was glaringly obvious that many women who have changed their names have a deep conflict about the true motivation behind their decision and the convenient excuses they present to the world. The blokes were just as illogical. And angry.

Why would anyone care what I think? Who'd give a monkey's about what a stranger writing in a newspaper would think about their choice? If someone had a go at something I'd decided to do, I wouldn't give a rat's. I'm happy with my choices.

I don't give a stuff what you do. I'm just paid to write what I think. There's no gun to your head. Turn the page. If you can't stand the heat, read the *Herald Sun*. Why bother trying to set me straight? All you've done is prove my point.

The defences were, well, defensive. "Well, it's just your father's surname anyway." No, it's not. It's mine. I was born with it. And if you follow that argument through, then you are not changing your surname to your husband's but to your father-in-law's.

"You are only a real family if you have the same surname." Wrong. If a family wants the same surname, why don't half of these families have the mother's surname? It seems only women have names that are hard to spell, they aren't attached to or they don't like. Not men. Odd. And convenient.

Women told me that their husbands would have been happy to change their surnames. But they didn't. I asked some of these blokes who, according to their wives, would have been happy to. They either said. "No, I wouldn't have but don't tell her" or just shuffled their feet and muttered, "I dunno, probably." You can say what you like now the deal is done.

I did a few radio interviews, and the callers were a real eye-opener. Men told me they agreed with me totally then proudly said: "I *told* my wife she didn't *have to* change her name," or "I *let* her keep her name but the kids *had to have* my surname." Where do I start?

It's a choice, but what's informing this choice is the issue. Why is it that it's "just easier" for "the wife" to change her name in almost 100 per cent of situations? It's easier for many not to take on convention and consequently reveal the depths of dormant patriarchy among their nearest and dearest. Then it's easier still to say: "It's just easier."

The stories I have heard of a backlash towards some women who kept their names are jaw-dropping. More women than you would think have confronted extremely angry reactions, with people telling them it is "illegal," "unethical" and "selfish" not to change their names. Others just ignore the woman's wishes and address her as Mrs He.

It's the mindless default setting, the convenient and flimsy excuses, the extreme defensiveness and the lack of rationality that's the worry. The personal is political. Surnames don't need to be uniform. Our society can cope with an equal mix of families with the male's surname, the female's, both, hyphenated (either mother's or father's surname first), male kids with one surname, female kids with the other and new family names. Bureaucracy can cope – but can you?

My theory? Many women want the same name as their children. They know their husband won't change or they don't want him to change (for fear of him being branded henpecked and/or her a femonazi), and they are certain that he won't accept the children having her surname or hyphenating. So change it is. And everything stays the same.

Childbirth I

Australia's caesarean rate of more than 30 per cent is disgraceful. The World Health Organisation recommends a caesarean rate of under 15 per cent, and the First World countries closest to that are the Netherlands (13.6 per cent) and Finland (16.1 per cent) – countries that have legislated one-on-one midwife care and have a medical culture that supports it.

The world's best and safest care for low-risk pregnancies is one-on-one midwife care. This care has been recommended by countless investigations and studies because it drastically cuts rates of unnecessary caesareans and other negative outcomes. Since New Zealand made sweeping legislation on birth choices 13 years ago, the percentage of women there who choose midwifery care has risen from 14 per cent to 80 per cent. There are sound medical reasons for caesareans, but not 30 per cent worth. Some women and babies are being ripped off.

How can the "too posh to push" consider that they are making an informed choice when the president of the Royal Australian and New Zealand College of Obstetricians and Gynaecologists, Chris Tippett, is on record saying that "the risks of caesarean for the mother are significantly greater, particularly if she has more than one caesarean. And secondly, it is very doubtful that there is any protective effect for the baby and there may be a significant disadvantage to the babies."

Answer? Negative optimism. Which is basically "it won't happen to me."

Last year a US study of more than 5 million births found that babies born by medically unnecessary caesareans were three times as likely to die in the newborn period as those born vaginally.

Professor James King, chairman of a ministerial advisory council on infant health, recommends strict guidelines on caesareans for private and public hospitals: "Caesareans divert funds from normal childbirth, but if you are operating in a private, for-profit system there is no disincentive to put a ceiling on that."

Dr Andrew Child, head of obstetrics at Royal Prince Alfred Hospital, has found that obstetricians in private practice fear legal action if they refuse a caesarean and the woman then has a problem birth. "They say, 'If someone asks, we just go along with it.'"

Many women are sucked in by the idea of a specialist because they want to be special. You hear a lot of, "My obstetrician said that if I hadn't had a caesarean I would have died." Of course they are going to say that. Show me an obstetrician who has performed a caesarean and then said, "I'm sorry, you actually could have delivered vaginally."

For many women, having a caesarean birth is like going to France and not seeing the Eiffel Tower. They suffer guilt, loss, anger, grief and depression because of feelings that they were bullied, coerced and manipulated at their most vulnerable. Many feel conned and cheated by "defensive medicine," which is generally the route taken so that if legal action arises they can say, "At least I did something."

I spent a day recently calling six hospitals asking for statistics on their birthing practices. I was greeted with, "Who did you say you were? And where are you calling from? And why do you want these statistics?" To which I replied, "To be informed." I was then told, "They're confidential and we generally don't give them out to the public."

Women generally make their decisions based on information from their peers. The majority will simply choose the same care that the majority of their family and friends choose.

So why won't the Federal government legislate for safer births with better outcomes for mothers, babies and society on the whole? Birth practices that would save the taxpayers millions of dollars?

Tony Abbott is too gutless to take on the doctors, because the doctors don't want their profits or power eroded. The mere suggestion that the government might take away their honey pot and power stick would have the AMA inciting panic and scaremongering. It would alienate voters because the public will always believe doctors over politicians.

It is difficult to dismantle the deeply entrenched cultural status that doctors have of being gods. They can't all be that smart; a fair whack of them vote Liberal. If they are so informed and so infallible, why do some doctors drink-drive, smoke cigarettes, have obesity problems or take recreational drugs? Negative optimism fuelled by a deep sense of superiority.

The Cochrane Collaboration, an international, independent not-for-profit organisation dedicated to providing information about the effects of healthcare, offers this conclusion in its *Guide to Effective Care in Pregnancy and Childbirth*: "It is inherently unwise, and perhaps unsafe, for women with normal pregnancies to be cared for by an obstetric specialist even if the required personnel are available."

I rest my case.

Childbirth II

When I mentioned to people that I was going to write an article on the large number of unnecessary caesareans, I was amused and alarmed by the extraordinary number of first responses that were, "You know that you're really going to upset the doctors." Well, I had better not say anything then.

Other people described me as "brave." Should I be worried that a gang of obstetricians will drive round in their BMWs, tilt their heads, look over their glasses at me and then burn down my house?

Good question. Who do I think I am? A consumer. An interested observer. A person who has heard hundreds of birth stories and experienced my own. A plain girl, not that clever, grew up on Struggle Street and constantly questioned anything labelled "the done thing." I found, more often than not, that behind these "done things" were people who had a vested interest in misleading, controlling and manipulating for their own personal gain.

For me to even question, let alone challenge, the process, culture or practices of the medical profession was met with: "How very dare you? Who do you think you are, young lady?" But for every member of the medical profession prepared to go on the record defending the current rate of caesareans and interventions, others have contacted me privately, encouraging me as being right on the money.

And how about that term "doctor-bashing"? How is doctor-questioning doctor-bashing? The medical and scientific community is an amazingly creative organic world full of curious people constantly questioning, researching and striving for better outcomes. It seems that you can't contribute to the debate unless you're in the club. But with birth, pregnancy and human lives, we're all in the club.

Even in my own article, I used quotes from doctors to fortify my own argument. Had I used terms such as wisdom, confidence, experience, spiritual journey, rite of passage, anecdotes and "the general vibe," I would have been disregarded as a mad, tree-hugging hippie.

Caesareans are like four-wheel drives. People who need to have them can't understand why anyone would choose to have them. Despite statistics and proof, some people will make a choice because they feel safer. Feeling safe is not always the same thing as being safe.

The culture of fear is not simply a fad. Human beings' brains are hardwired to feel fear more keenly than reason. It's a primal response that kept us alive in the highland plains of East Africa in 100,000 BC. In his essay "The Psychology of Security," Bruce Schneier says a brain hardwired to feel fear strongly "works great if you're a lizard or a lion. Some scary things are not really as risky as they seem, and others are better handled by staying in the scary situation to set up a more advantageous future response. This means there's an evolutionary advantage to being able to hold off the reflexive fight-or-flight response while you work out a more sophisticated analysis of the situation and your options for handling it."

There is also the culture of cash. Many people feel that the more they pay for something the more superior it is. The births of my three children cost $18, $14 and $8. That money was spent on parking. The care I received and the births I experienced were wonderful.

The government needs to bankroll midwives' insurance and give them a Medicare provider number. Women will be able to choose one-on-one midwife care and then the idea of birthing without a doctor will not be seen as radical, alternative or weird, but mainstream. If the pregnancy becomes high-risk, the midwife can refer the woman to an obstetrician. The statistics will get better and the culture will change.

The bottom line is not nice but it's true. Babies and mothers will continue to die during childbirth. We need to ensure the safest practices possible. The infant and maternal death rate in Australia has basically remained unchanged, yet the rate of caesareans has skyrocketed and caesareans have a higher rate of maternal and infant deaths. Babies and mothers are now dying for different reasons. Reasons that could be prevented.

I wrote last week's article for those women who had placed faith in their birthing choices and then felt sucked in, ripped off and angry by the outcome. Women who were told that they were too small, too old, too slow-labouring or that their babies were too big, too small, had funny-shaped heads, were in the wrong position, were overdue, were upside down or were multiples and told that they had no other choice. Only to find out later that they did have other choices.

A movie due out later this year called *Pregnant in America* is poised to be the *Fahrenheit 9/11*, *An Inconvenient Truth* and *Super Size Me* of birthing practices. The culture is changing and about bloody time.

Saudi Arabian Women I

This is not about Islam. I have experienced far more decent behaviour from Muslim men on Sydney Road than I ever experienced from the leering and threatening bogans I grew up with in Reservoir. And far more decent than the born-to-rule private school boys reeking of misogyny and entitlement pressing up against me at the bar of the Geebung Polo Club.

Women of the Holy Kingdom is, on one hand, a terrifying reminder of the oppressive regime of gender apartheid to which women are subjected in Saudi Arabia. On the other, there is encouraging news about the country's emerging women's movement. Sharmeen Obaid Chinoy, raised in a progressive Muslim society in Pakistan, spent four weeks in the Holy Kingdom making this fascinating, well-balanced documentary that chilled me to the bone.

Obaid Chinoy was permitted to make the documentary as long as she was escorted by a male chaperone provided by the government at all times and wore the *abaya* (head-to-toe black covering) to prevent the possibility of temptation and moral corruption.

Under Saudi rule, an unmarried adult woman is the ward of her father, a married woman is the ward of her husband and a widowed woman is the ward of her sons. To obtain a passport, check into a hotel or be admitted to a hospital, women need the permission of their male guardian. Women are forbidden to drive and are segregated in public. That's the bad news.

Good news: the Saudi royal family is committed to reform and keen to grant more rights to women.

Bad news: there is strong opposition from the religious clerics.

Good news: there are now conferences on women's issues.

Feels good. Feels like progress.

Then, on the evening of the conference, as Obaid Chinoy and her crew film, they are hassled by the religious police (officially called the Committee for the Propagation of Virtue and the Condemnation of Vice). They accuse the all-women camera crew of attracting male attention and demand to know why the television company did not send a male crew. Although the crew has government documentation, the crew's male chaperone sorts it out by promising they will be more discreet.

This documentary is a ride the whole way through. One minute I found myself laughing at an irreverent Saudi comedy show that "openly addresses the conflicts between traditional Saudi rules and modern society."

The next thing I hear is what sounds like Stockholm Syndrome, as a confident young married university student says she doesn't mind having to ask her husband for permission for everything.

Furthermore, Suzan, a (female) hospital administrator, tells how she left a job because the dress code was too liberal (the private hospital she was working at forbade women covering their faces). She goes on to explain that females do not always have good judgement because of their "hormones."

No, this is not about Islam. This is about fundamentalism and extremism. This show is a must-see.

But more next week …

Saudi Arabian Women II

As I was saying last week, *Women of the Holy Kingdom* is a great documentary about the women of Saudi Arabia. Watch it, but don't think that this is what all Muslim women are or how all Muslim women live. That would be like watching *Big Brother* and concluding that all Australians are dickheads.

In January, SBS screened the documentary *Veiled Ambition,* to which the producers are filming a sequel. The opening scene shows Frida Dakiz wearing a hijab and sunglasses, fanging around in her car smoking a ciggie. Chattily, Ms Dakiz says: "Chicks without scarves are probably nice as well."

After winning $4000 in a radio competition, the "little Aussie battler in a scarf" opened a shop in Brunswick that she hoped would be a fashion mecca for Muslim women. When the hip Islamic chic didn't move as well as hoped, she eschewed the burqas and hijabs for Hollywood-styled gowns.

Ms Dakiz, a feminist, returned to work when her daughter was a month old. She and her husband agreed that she would stay in Melbourne to expand her business while he built their house in Sydney. She is a funny, loveable and down-to-earth loudmouth who has a thriving business of four stores. My favourite moment was when, bustling around the kitchen, she turned to camera and said: "Cooking roast chicken for Ramadan. How Aussie is that?"

One of the highly educated women interviewed in *Women of the Holy Kingdom*, Dr Thuraya Arrayed, is thrilled by the progress of women but cautions: "We don't want to be mutilated versions of what happened in the West."

Which is a good idea. And if you don't believe me, check out the atrocities and human disfigurement committed on *Extreme Makeover* in the name of vanity and ratings.

This show is rated PG; it should be rated ABC – Atrocious But Compelling. These rather plain folk who have, admittedly, been hit with the ordinary stick, expose themselves to humiliation and degradation for our amusement. They tell us how difficult their life has been being ugly/old/ungrateful and how their life will be turned around after their brow-lift, chin implant, eye-tuck, nose job, gum recontouring and porno breast-implants to improve "self-esteem."

After surgery, exercise, new hair and clothes, friends clap, family weep and children ask: "Where's Mummy?" But it's not always happily ever after. A woman allegedly killed herself after her sister was dropped as a contestant.

Deleese Williams was promised a Cinderella-like makeover and the producers forced her family to bag her looks on camera. The night before her dental surgery she was dropped from the show because the recovery wouldn't fit the show's schedule. Ms Williams is reported as saying her sister Kellie committed suicide because of her guilt at the comments she had made about her sister's appearance. Saudi Arabia doesn't look that extreme, after all.

Chastity

I'm a bit obsessed with a story. And no, it's not the one about the New Zealand parents who want to name their child 4real. Wait until Victoria Beckham gets a whiff of that one. She'll be knocked up quicker than you can say "sour-faced, skeletal publicity junkie." Maybe she should name a kid after what she did all pregnancy: 8nothing 4months 2diet.

And no, it's not "Stab victim continued masturbating." Although that little gem did remain the most viewed article for days and days until the headline was changed to "Stab victim continued sex act" and then it plummeted to number two.

It's a story about a 16-year-old girl in Britain. Her name is Lydia Playfoot (and no, that's not the story, but as you read on you will have a little chortle to yourself that young Lydia has the name of a porn star). She wears a silver "purity" ring on her finger to show the world her commitment to sexual abstinence before marriage.

When Mr Right comes along, they'll have an ownership ceremony and live happily ever after until they pass over to be with God Almighty and are joined in eternity. For eternity. It won't happen overnight, but it will happen.

Millais School in West Sussex allows Sikh and Muslim students to wear headscarves and religious bracelets but will not allow our Lydia to wear her ring of chastity. Why? Well, they consider that wearing a chastity ring is not an integral part of the Christian faith. Lydia's had a gutful and is suing the school in the High Court, claiming that, hold on tight folks, not allowing her to wear the ring is a breach of human rights. Is this what the world has come to? Kill me now.

I love this story because I don't believe in God, I don't believe in chastity and I don't believe in people called Lydia Playfoot. And I love the hypocrisy of a school that evaluates some mumbo-jumbo as legitimate and other examples as, well, a bit of a crock.

Lydia belongs to a movement called Silver Ring Thing, which is all about "saving yourself" before marriage. Lydia's parents are central to the UK chapter of this cult/fellowship/loyalty program. Silver Ring Thing originated in, you guessed it, America. If it's not here already, keep your eyes out for the Aussie version, Jim's Silver Ring Thing. US happy-clappy religions love cooking up a bit of sizzle with their "What would Jesus do?" tattoos, their "intelligent design" and their "true love waits." True love may wait, but nothing can stop teenage hormones. Apart from the threat of eternal damnation. That doesn't always work, but it's worth a red-hot go.

We all know that virginity was invented to keep women under the thumb so that blokes could feel confident they were leaving their land and cash to their actual kid.

Let's face it, virginity is only for chicks. Sure, when you

ask people they'll tell you that it applies to men too. But it's a bit offhand, a bit unconvincing, a bit "nudge, nudge, wink, wink." Ladies, knees together. Guys? Oh, all right, off you go, you rascals. But don't tell your mother.

Marriage doesn't work. One-third of first marriages and two-thirds of second marriages end in divorce. If marriage were a car, we would have taken it to the wreckers and started using taxis. Oh, that's right, we have. Hello to all the de factos reading this. Chastity doesn't work either, but it is a valuable indication of intelligence and gullibility.

And why a chastity ring? Why go halfway? Why not a full-on chastity belt? Why not shave their heads? Why not just lock themselves up in cages and enter into an arranged marriage at 15?

Why does Lydia have to show the world her commitment? Remember the Catholic scapular? Nice little fabric postage stamp that your mum pinned to your singlet. Discreet, classy, understated. Dress it up with a mantilla, dress it down with a set of rosary beads. Kept you safe. Another great example of restraint is the Mormon "temple garment." A neck-to-knee kind of arrangement worn under your clothes. Has to be white. Won't work if it's another colour. Again, nothing showy. What does it do? Well, it protects you against the powers of evil.

If they allow Lydia's magic ring of virginity, what next? "Sorry, sir, I can't take off this headband because it represents my lifetime commitment to responsible meat-handling."

Let her wear the chastity ring, I say. Let them all wear their scarves, garments, yarmulkas, hairshirts or magic cockroach-testicles in small hemp bags around their necks. Just let me wear my T-shirt that reads: "I don't believe in anything apart from the fact that you're all barking mad."

Blokey TV

I wish I were a guy writing this. Because I'm a chick, it'll sound like sour grapes. A bit "nyeh, nyeh nyeh, it's not fair, nyeh, nyeh, nyeh, there's nothing for us ladies, nyeh, nyeh, nyeh."

But it's not just girls, but guys, too, who are disturbed that Australian television has descended into a full-on buck's night in Moe.

TV has always been blokey. Australian television particularly so. But Australian television now is so blokey that the viewer can't help but wonder if Sheikh Taj al-Din al-Hilali and Hugh Hefner are coming up with the content.

The extreme blokeyness of Australian commercial television in particular (but not exclusively) is terrifying. The only thing more terrifying is that no one is saying anything about it. Have we simply become the frogs in the boiling water? The temperature being knocked up ever so slightly, ever so slowly that people don't even notice?

"What are you talking about, love? There are chicks on telly. That Livinia Nixon. That Fifi Whatshername. That lady who does the Brand Power ads. And that Maxine McKew. What? Gone into politics? Well, there's Jana Wendt. Sorry? Whatever. Stop whingeing. Chicks aren't funny. And they're not smart. Get me a beer and pass me a remote, it's time for Ralph TV."

This warped gender equation has become so normalised that if I mention it people roll their eyes and try to set me straight by pointing out the one woman on a program of five or more men, who says pretty much bugger-all. The normalisation of this gender apartheid is almost as dangerous as the token female employed to create an illusion of equality.

Don't just look at the small number of females that you see on screen and the tiny age bracket that they come from, but what they are employed to do, how they are forced to look and what they are expected to, sorry, I mean allowed to, say. You'll find that in most cases you have women acting like girls.

You'll see very few women acting or looking like adult women. This is because any person with a vagina combined with passionate and strong opinions is labelled shrill, overwrought, needing a Bex and a lie-down or, more hilarious still, "needing a slap." Or as the network execs would say, "a bit too ABC."

The very few women in power in this ghetto of 1950s gender stereotypes are playing the blokes' game. Not only has feminism not reached the commercial stations; neither has evolution. Cro-Magnons run wild, raping and pillaging our culture and the realities of the young and the impressionable. It's an Aussie BBQ: the blokes are turning snags, bragging about cars, sport and chicks, and the girls are fussing about in the kitchen, whipping up a sponge and saying, "Lovely bean salad, Nola!"

Channel Nine is the Saudi Arabia of the television world. Segregation is thriving and I am fairly sure that sharia law will be introduced at the station any day soon. You will not see any woman on screen who looks over the age of 25.

Mia Freedman's recent departure from Nine was not surprising. She was employed to provide a woman's touch at the channel. They expected her to plonk a few vases of flowers around the place. She came up with *The Catch-Up*. What would make anyone think that female viewers were after some half-baked, single-sex rip-off just for the ladies? Put me on the Nine board. I'll be boning faster than a butcher's apprentice on a Friday arvo.

Beef for the men, chicken for the ladies. "Vegetarian? What are ya? A lesbian?" *The Footy Show*? 9.30 weeknights. *The Catch-Up*? Weekday lunchtime. How hilarious in this day and age to program a show exclusively for women, featuring an all-women line-up, in the middle of the day. As if we're all home doing the ironing while hubby's at the office and the secret women's business has to go on during the day. Because in the evening women aren't allowed to use the television; father has to watch his shows, with a hound at his feet and a pipe in his mouth and mother performing fellatio. If they'd named it *The Scrag Fight*, it might still be on air.

Australian TV is in a diabolical state. Audiences are turning on their heels and going elsewhere. And good on them. I urge you all to switch off and run as fast as you can to send the strongest message possible.

If nothing is done soon, we will have no Australian content left and our skilled and passionate television practitioners will all be making television on Australian soil for other countries. Our stories will no longer be told and our kids will say "butt" not "bum," dial 911 and when questioned, "plead the Fifth Amendment."

The current Ken and Barbie reality of Australian television is disastrous for us all. And it's getting worse.

International Women's Day I

Dear lady doctor, woman driver, female boss, beauty queen, drunk mole, daughter-in-law, prima donna, old maid, fag hag, debutante, femme fatale, gold digger, hostess with the mostest, nymphomaniac, Playmate of the year, local bike, Avon lady, innocent virgin, mail-order bride, jezebel, girl next door, ex-wife, cheap hooker, shrinking violet, single mother, spinster, trophy wife, headmistress, dumb blonde, damsel in distress, bridesmaid, bearded lady, pushy bitch and any girl who has ever jumped out of a cake,

May I wish you all the best on International Women's Day and say, on behalf of all the rough-headed yobbos who think that feminists are all stuck-up frigid lezzos: No Root, No Ride.

You *have* come a long way, baby! These days dildos are a girl's best friend, gentlemen prefer blondes with a secondary education and hell hath no fury like a woman who has just lost her libel case thanks to the inexperienced solicitor briefing her. It ain't over till the fat lady arrives before the creche closes, gets the kids to bed, pays the babysitter and manages to pick up the take-away Thai for her and her partner to eat in the car before the information night on the impact of the GST on dual-income households begins. A woman's work is never done unless she employs a personal assistant and for the love of a good woman you will be required to sign a pre-nuptial agreement. You'll be pleased to know that the hand that rocks the cradle still receives very little gratitude indeed.

What's a nice girl like me doing on a page like this? Making my own money, which I put into my own bank account, which I spend on what I bloody well feel like. By being funny, and swearing. Shit. See? That's feminism.

We chicks are halfway there the way I see it, but do keep in mind that Barry Jones is a viable long term partner the way I see it as well. As soon as we have a quiz show hosted by a mature, patronising woman whose sidekick is a tanned, blond, wordless airhead bloke, we'll be on our way. When the day comes that a man goes to work and his male colleagues ask "who's looking after your kids?" the hard work will have begun to pay off. When we no longer need women's studies to supplement the gaping cavernous hole that is our participation in history, I will believe that the suffragettes' fight is over. As soon as the scoreboard at Wimbledon no longer specifies whether the female playing is a Miss or a Mrs, while male players have no title at all, I will believe that my little sisters may grow up in a world without eating disorders.

So today, my friend, have a shandy, a cream sherry or a shot of moselle, and rejoice in the journey of the women who have won, the women who've been beaten and the women who have told you that you've tucked your skirt into your pantyhose.

International Women's Day II

"My daughter is going through a phase of wearing jeans that are so tight she can't bend her knees in them. I have a go at her and say, 'Can't you wear something else? And please wear a belt because I don't want to see your butt crack when you bend over.'"

That's what Madonna said in the latest issue of British *Elle*.

You remember Madonna? She used to be about empowering herself through porn and pointy bras. Now she rides ponies and wears tweed. And probably says the words "golly" and "utterly" a lot. But despite being considered a massive joke, she is filthy, stinking rich and she can do, think or buy whatever she pleases. Including children.

Tomorrow is International Women's Day. There go half the readers. And to celebrate, I'm off shopping for shoes and I'm going to take the lids off jars myself. The truth is that the perfect International Women's Day for most (not all) women reading this paper would be finding out that their partner's ex-girlfriend had put on 10 kilos, aged 20 years and was last seen wearing fawn slacks. As opposed to the average woman in the world, whose perfect International Women's Day would be a safe roof over her head, a warm meal in her belly and not having her head punched in.

Is tomorrow simply an opportunity for middle-class women like me to drink chardonnay and air kiss? Has International Women's Day, sandwiched between Answer Your Cat's Question Day on 22 January and International Feng Shui Awareness Day, 8 April, facilitated one woman procuring a safe legal abortion, taught one girl to read or prevented the infanticide of one baby who had the misfortune to be born female?

I'm torn. There are as many ways to be a woman as there are women walking this earth and as many forms of feminism as feminists. So where should we focus our energies to further the cause of equality for all? Tribally or globally? Or simply by attempting to set a good example?

Some say that education is the priority. Others will say that it's preventing domestic violence, promoting religious tolerance, dealing with body image, confronting the problems of indigenous women, while others say that first we need to focus on how we raise boys.

I have three boys. The upside is that I feel like a goddess. The downside is that the toilet does smell like an animal enclosure. The boys say breasts not boobs, they have hyphenated surnames with my surname first and all three have worn pink. Cleaning, cooking, caring and emotional literacy are also included in the curriculum. How much difference will these efforts make? Who knows? But when you don't know what to do, do anything. And I suppose that makes International Women's Day something.

Considering there is no status in being a parent or carer, let's at least give these skilled and dedicated individuals wads of cash and a fancy name, such as "domestic engineer" or "early childhood development specialist." Seriously. And let's stop discussing maternity leave and go in swinging for *paid* parenting, *paid* grandparenting and *paid* caring.

People bemoan that there are too few women in boardrooms. That won't change until women don't have to sacrifice their family lives, their private lives and their spiritual lives to do it. Because most won't. To most women, no amount of money and power is worth that. But the few women who want to work insane hours in the cut-throat and hateful corporate world that corrodes the soul, dilutes relationships and endangers health should have the right to a heart attack before the age of 50, just as much as any bloke.

To dismantle the boys' clubs that possess, distribute and create the power, we need positive discrimination, family-friendly legislation and a massive cultural shift. Which I doubt will happen in any of our lifetimes.

It is International Women's Day, so I wonder how they celebrate it in Pakistan, Iraq, Iran and Afghanistan. Is it a bit of: "Can't give you access to education, financial autonomy and basic healthcare but here, have a sticker"? Maybe in Saudi Arabia they let the women out of their cages for the day.

An estimated 20 million unsafe abortions are performed worldwide every year, resulting in the deaths of 70,000 women. Each year an estimated 2 million girls suffer genital mutilation. Twenty to 50 per cent of women experience some degree of domestic violence during marriage. The majority of women earn on average about 75 per cent of the pay of males for the same work.

In most countries, women work approximately twice the unpaid time men do. Of the world's nearly 1 billion illiterate adults, two-thirds are women. Women hold 11.7 per cent of the seats in the world's parliaments. Nearly 70 per cent of the world's 1.3 billion poor people are women. Between 75 and 80 per cent of the world's 27 million refugees are women and children.

And just so you know, International Men's Day is 19 November.

Vasectomy

With all this war, violence and aggression, I want to write something light and witty, but I'm not sure how to start. It could go something like:

A) The birth story of my last child has done the rounds of so many dinner parties, backyard barbies and family fun days that it has proved beyond a shadow of a doubt that we have no life beyond having children. (Just in case you are one of the three people who haven't heard, it was a two-hour water birth with no stitches. I pulled him out of the water [which apparently looked like a magic trick] and cut the cord myself while sitting in the birthing pool [which could easily have been mistaken for the scene of a shark attack].) So, in an attempt to prove that we do have a life beyond having children, we have decided to embark on a new project that also involves genitals, discomfort and bruising for up to a week. And no, we are not going to Mardi Gras.

Or

B) My partner is having a vasectomy next week.

To fill you in, we now have three boys. We refuse to purchase a people-mover, so the man of my dreams (well, he certainly is now) is joining the V-squad next week. That's right, he's having the snip. Actually it's a puncture and then a snip and then possibly a bit of oozing. That's according to the literature and you know they always make it sound better in the brochure.

Before you get all uppity about me taking the micky out of my partner having his genitals mutilated, let me tell you that:

1. He forced me to write this article (we've just seen what the V-man charges).

2. I've made a living out of my own genitals being mutilated for the last seven years, thank you very much.

3. This topic was fair game after he had his initial consultation on 14 February. I received a note written on the urologist's letterhead saying, "For Valentine's Day, your partner has booked in for a vasectomy." Which was nice because at least it wasn't another Breville Snack and Sandwich Maker.

Do keep in mind that he is only having this vasectomy so that people will think we still have sex. I am thrilled that we are finishing our family in such a definite fashion. It makes it almost a ritual. *We* are having the vasectomy, so I am going along to support him. And also because, just between you and me, I've never been one to miss a good photo opportunity. In keeping with the theme of our last birth, I am trying to convince him to have a water vasectomy. I think that without drugs it could be an ending-all-life-giving experience.

When we tell people, they all say, "Ooohhh, isn't it supposed to be painful?" Have they heard about CHILDBIRTH? It was completely his decision in the end. All I said was, "Well, you can go and get it done professionally, or alternatively I can do it here at home." Everyone loves to think that I am the ball-breaker (no pun intended, but you've got to admit it was pretty funny), but the truth is that it's his idea. He doesn't see it as a threat to his masculinity; on the contrary, he feels he doesn't have a choice. "Ladies, stand back, it could go off at any time without warning. I'm so potent I could fertilise an Easter egg." After four pregnancies in four years he could come under suspicion of harbouring a weapon of mass conception.

He froze some sperm in the end. When he told me that he needed a semen sample I just told him to take the shower curtain.

Carry on populating this vast brown land, my friends, because, with three kids, our cue's back in the rack for good.

Circumcision

No one seems to be able to explain to me why the circumcision of baby boys is not considered child abuse. Why in 2007 is it still acceptable for parents to have their babies' foreskin ripped off? How can it be legal, let alone ethical, for any human being to choose for another human being's body to be irreversibly mutilated? No medical reason, no rational thought and in many cases no anaesthetic. Just because.

I suggest that we should ban the use of the term circumcision and force people to use the term genital mutilation. Because that's what it is. It's not "a personal choice," because that person is not making a choice. It's a human rights abuse.

The We Circumcised for Religious Reasons Camp justifies genital mutilation by citing religion. They embrace the parts of religious texts that suit them and dismiss the ones that don't. And when I say "they," not all of them do. Many believers I know have all applied a little rational thought to the equation and just decided not to inflict unnecessary pain on their child or expose them to avoidable risk. They've decided to file that bit of the Holy Book with the other things that just don't fit, like selling your daughter into slavery or killing your neighbour if they work on the Sabbath.

What kind of God would disapprove of you, stop loving you or not give you eternal life if you *don't* mutilate your child's genitals? That doesn't sound like a nice kind of God. And what caring community would shun you, judge you or ostracise you for *not* inflicting genital mutilation on your child?

Then we have the We Circumcised Our Boys So They Would Look the Same as Their Father Camp. Sure, it's not fair for me to pick on people less fortunate in the brains department than the rest of us, but when they are subjecting innocent children to genital mutilation I'm going in swinging. I'm not going to bother asking the hard question – "Why do you need them to look like their father?" –

because you cannot reason with something that has come not from reason but from mindlessness.

I ask the So They Look the Same as Their Father Camp: why stop there? If you want them to look the same as their father, dye their hair, have them undergo cosmetic surgery and, if the father has any tattoos or facial hair, sort that out too. Related to this camp is the We Circumcised Our Boys Because a Circumcised Penis Looks Nicer Camp. We are talking the shallow end of the intelligence pool here. How would they feel if they had had their nipples, nose or ears cut off by their parents because their parents thought "it looked nicer"? I must say that I do applaud these two camps for their frankness and honesty in revealing the most stunning stupidity. They could have done what other people do: decide for no rational reason, then join the We Circumcised Our Boys for Health and Hygiene Despite Looking Closely at the Research Camp.

I have read the various studies suggesting that circumcision may reduce the risk of spreading HIV and cervical cancer. I have also read the studies disproving this myth. Here in first-world Australia all of these risks can be effectively and safely managed with condoms and cleanliness. That's right: frangers and face washers, rubbers and rubbing. Why would you expose children to an unnecessary medical procedure and all the risks that come with it when you could teach them how to clean themselves and use a condom? Because you can, I suppose. If we're following this logic, let's remove all children's teeth to prevent them getting fillings.

Unless of course there is a sound medical reason to circumcise. And when I say sound, I mean sound as in last resort. I don't mean that you walk into a general practitioner with a seven-year-old with a constricted foreskin that is not retracting and walk out with a referral to a surgeon to have your child's genitals mutilated. As a family I know could have.

One of their sons had that very problem. They were offered a referral to a surgeon to have him circumcised. They didn't like the sound of that. Luckily they didn't have private health insurance and were given a referral to the Royal Children's Hospital, where they saw a general paediatric surgeon. Or, as their son referred to her, a Dick Doctor. Yes, she said, he could be circumcised, but she was having great success using an ointment available over the counter from the chemist. Three days later, he had a retracting foreskin. And two years later, he still does. The wonders of a health service on a budget as opposed to a private business. So if he wants to get himself circumcised as an adult, that's his choice. And he'll have that choice. Because when you circumcise someone you can't uncircumcise them. Just ask the Reclaim the Foreskin movement.

Valentine's Day

Unless you're in a long-term relationship, you have no good reason not to know that it's Valentine's Day today. Are you one of those people who love nothing more than a walk along the beach reading love sonnets to your precious? Or would you rather be home watching the latest Van Damme movie with a family-size super-supreme? Not quite sure? Let me help you find out …

The purpose of Valentine's Day is:
a) To keep florists in business.

b) To provide my partner with another opportunity to convince me that I'm being taken for granted.
c) To enable me to feel superior to all those mindless suburban peasants brainwashed by capitalism.
d) To help ugly people get laid.

Do you believe in Valentine's Day?
a) Only if I get something.
b) Only if I get something.
c) Only if I get something.
d) All of the above.

Physical love between two people occurs when:
a) They are in love.
b) They are pissed.
c) They don't have children.
d) The guttering gets cleaned out and painted.

If you are attracted to someone, a good opening line is:
a) What star sign are you?
b) Grab your coat, you've won.
c) You look like you'd go right off.
d) Ever tripped over a tree trunk? How about a root?

You had the date of your dreams. You wake up the next morning with:
a) Two dozen champagne-coloured roses.
b) A sore head.
c) Genital herpes.
d) A person who looks like Ugly Dave Gray saying that they didn't realise that it was legal to do that with a goat.

I read *Men Are from Mars, Women Are from Venus*:
a) Because I'm interested in relationships.
b) To stop my partner from hassling me.
c) Because I thought it was a porno.
d) To see what crap that creepy little midget who wrote it made millions out of.

If I was going to be stranded on a desert island, I would take:
a) My partner, a candelabra and a violinist.
b) A deep breath and thank the Lord above for taking pity on me.
c) An inflatable companion named Randy, a box of pornos and a water bed.
d) My extensive collection of Tim Tams, my bucket bong and half-a-dozen gerbils.

Complete this sentence: "Love is …"
a) Togetherness.
b) Over-rated.
c) Expensive.
d) Very hard to get out of leather upholstery.

I call my partner:
a) My love.
b) Tiger funny fluffy cutie pants.
c) The Beast.
d) After I have sex with my secretary.

Porn is:
a) Something to do with chess.
b) A cheap night out.

c) Difficult to hide from the cleaning lady.
d) 80 per cent of my weekly spending.

A perfect first date is:
a) A romantic dinner for two, French champagne and a walk on the beach.
b) A game of pool, a couple of glasses of merlot and deconstructing Pasolini films until dawn.
c) About $100 an hour but cheaper in Asia.
d) Half a slab, minimum chips and a Saturday arvo at Pick-a-Part.

You believe that love can be summed up by which of the following sayings:
a) Absence makes the heart grow fonder.
b) If you can't be with the one you love, stalk them.
c) It's not the size of the dog in the fight it's the size of the fight in the dog.
d) What doesn't kill you makes you stronger.

Your favourite love song is:
a) "When a Man Loves a Woman."
b) "Sexual Healing."
c) "I Like It Both Ways."
d) "Up There Cazaly."

You think it is appropriate to fart (pass wind) in front of your partner:
a) Never.
b) If you are watching television and it's a really good bit.
c) In order to increase your pleasure during the act of love.
d) Just so they know you still care.

Mostly As:
You are the most cliché-ridden traditionalist imaginable. You think men should propose, women should wear dresses more and that your parents don't have genitals. You love lace, have a picture of you partner on your desk and have good family values. Those who don't hate you are bored by you or are related to you.

Mostly Bs:
You go along with the whole romantic thing because your partner believes in it and you can't be stuffed arguing. You were in love once but when you brought them home to meet the family they carved their name in your dad's forehead. If you have a partner they are sad and ugly, and if you don't they will be.

Mostly Cs:
You are what is known as a reconstructed new romantic. You believe in Tantric sex and equality if it will get you a shag. You like to use incense, massage oil and mirrors and occasionally you use them on your partners as well. You don't have a little black book, you have a little black White Pages. Basically, you're a root-rat, a wanker or somebody's pimp.

Mostly Ds:
You'll be pleased to know that St Valentine was beaten with clubs and afterwards beheaded in the third century. If you were saying it with flowers you'd be sending triffids. You hate anything cute, sentimental or traditional – especially if it costs money. You are what is technically known as sad, twisted and bitter. The last time you felt love was during a conjugal visit.

The three-episode challenge

*

McLeod's Daughters

I started thinking that I should write more about Australian drama. Support the industry, promote local content, plug Aussie talent. So I watched three episodes of *McLeod's Daughters*. And it's shithouse. But let's face it, I hated it before I turned it on. And you hate it, too, even though you've never watched it. And you hate the people who watch it, even though you've never met them. Don't worry, the people who watch *McLeod's Daughters* aren't reading this because they are having a sleepover at Cindy's place, straddling a broom and making horsey noises or writing "I love ponies 4 EVA!!!!" on their folders. So sit back and enjoy, as I confirm your presumptions and massage your prejudices again.

It's difficult to believe, but watching *McLeod's Daughters* was worse than I expected. This tribute to mediocrity and committee-created slop is a cross between *The Saddle Club* and a tampon advertisement. It's kind of Mills & Boon with horses but devoid of artistic merit. All 179 episodes. God help us.

Watching this badly written, poorly directed money-spinner made me sad/angry/bored/desperate to sit 'round a campfire singing "The Court of King Caractacus" in more or less equal proportions. The cast are not good-looking enough to be models but are deluded enough to think they can act. It's heterosexual, Caucasian spunks between 21 and 22 as far as the eye can see, apart from one really old woman, who was probably 24. She has powers to speak to the dead, which came in handy when one of the daughters was having visions and hearing voices. Which lead to this dialogue:

GIRL: There was a woman crying.

WOMAN: What kind of crying?

GIRL: [THINKS HARD] Sad.

Then it comes over all porno as one handsome stud says to another, "That looks like a big job, need a hand?" Turns out they're brothers. The dialogue is so bad, the acting so poor and the audience so stupid that excessive amounts of incidental music are necessary to indicate to the viewer when to feel happy, when to feel hopeful and when bad stuff is on its way.

It is very good at what it is. Which is shit. Death, birth, lost love, found love, explosions, ghosts and witness-protection programs; all with extremely high production values. If you like your acting like your tables, wooden and with four legs, tune into *McLeod's Daughters*.

This show does provide one valuable service: it gives these actors work, which prevents them inflicting their musical careers on the public.

Most people collapse on the couch every night and watch telly. I can assure you that if Channel Nine programmed *The Toe Jam of John Howard* at 7.30 pm on Wednesday they would still get 1.3 million viewers simply because it's between *Temptation* and *The Footy Show*.

Who's to blame? The people who make this homophobic, xenophobic, jingoistic crap or the people who encourage them by switching over? *The Biggest Loser* is not on Ten, it's on the couch watching *McLeod's Daughters*.

All Saints

OK readers, strap yourself in. To prove to you that television reviewing can be an extreme sport, I have given myself a Three-Episode Challenge. I'm pumped, I'm high fiving, I'm air punching and they are backing in the icy cold cans of Coke. There may be urine testing involved but that's OK, I'm no stranger to taking the piss.

The Challenge consists of me watching three episodes of all the 2007 Logie nominees for "Most Popular Drama." Last week it was a little pony porn with *Airheads on Horseback* (sorry, I mean *McLeod's Daughters*) and this week it's *All Saints*.

I have chanced upon the odd snippet of this Aussie-made hospital drama in the past and thought to myself, "It's a bit like *ER* but with ugly people." *ER* had George Clooney. *All Saints* has John Howard. Point made. Medical dramas have huge appeal because the opportunities for life and death are more feasible and with a bit of doctors-and-nurses thrown in, we're talking a licence to print TV guides.

Wealthy, self-funded retirees chat about their trips to Tuscany. Poor pensioners talk about their trips to casualty. I'll choose medical drama over any other kind faster than you can say, "80 mills of hyperthorax! Stat!" I wonder if these shows raise public awareness about illnesses – or do they just turn us all into hypochondriacs?

So with a glass of red in my left hand and a pewter goblet of truth in the other I say to you that, not only did I watch three episodes of *All Saints*, but I watched four. Because I enjoyed it.

You have Von Ryan, the gruff matron with the heart of gold, John Campion, the grumpy maverick head of emergency with the messy personal life, Dr Bianca Frost, the conniving bitch, Mike Vlasek, the brilliant surgeon with the substance-abuse problem and a young Doogie Howseresque Dr Bartholomew West, intern complete with knitted vests.

For fleeting moments it feels a bit "three stereotypes walked into a hospital" and there is the odd cheesy line; but, all in all (and I know you hate it when I don't hate something), it's good telly.

The story-lines are well executed, with intelligent and challenging subject matter, snappy dialogue and mostly fine acting. The partner of one of the doctors finds out that their baby has spina bifida and she decides to terminate the pregnancy against his will, interspersed with gay relationships, child abuse and an accident resulting in an internal decapitation.

Two of the directors of the episodes I watched were Daina Read and Nick Bufalo. Both are perfect examples of how experienced and versatile our television practitioners are. Both have extensive TV experience directing, writing and performing comedy and drama, which illustrates how, in our tiny industry, you have to be a Jack or Jill of all trades.

I don't know if it's always this good but I would watch *All Saints* for free.

Neighbours

I wasn't looking forward to watching *Neighbours*. I took a deep breath and reminded myself that I have undergone chemotherapy and given birth without drugs, so watching three episodes of *Neighbours* should be pretty similar. But with more fake tan.

I psyched myself up by chanting, "What doesn't kill you makes you stronger! What doesn't kill you makes you stronger!" And I kept reminding myself that it was my duty as a reviewer and as self-appointed Fairfax-funded ambassador for truth. It was going to be like pulling off a Band-Aid. Commit to it, make it fast and do it in the bath so it hurts less.

So I set up the laptop and hopped in the bath. That's right, I was watching *Neighbours* naked and wet. You want the truth? You can't handle the truth. It was time to brace myself. As the credits rolled and that familiar music excreted, I was very afraid.

But the show is hilarious. It's an absolute ball-tearer. This shouldn't have a Logie nomination for most popular drama, it should be cleaning up the comedy awards.

With episode titles like "Look Who's Stalking," "Just What the Doctor Frauded," "Quack of Beyond," "Give Priest a Chance" and "Assault and Pepper," this is the funniest thing that I have seen on Australian TV since they chained up a nana in a nursing home on *Today Tonight*.

Ramsay Street's still there. So too is Lasseter's pub and the coffee shop. And yes, Erinsborough is still a bizarre demographic blip of 20 size-eight teenage girls to every one person over 40.

Rowena Wallace plays a psychopath who makes scones and then locks a blonde girl in a room with a cradle, a clown and some unhingeing music-box lullaby. Stefan Dennis, as the moustache-twirling panto villain Paul Robinson, is a genius. I just wanted to yell out, "He's behind you! He's behind you!" It takes sheer brilliance to be able to act that badly. And Ian Smith (playing Harold Bishop) still talks as if he has a mouth full of marbles. This show is young people trying to act and old actors pretending not to.

I hear you writers tapping away, thinking, "Well if I have to write this crap, I am going to make sure people know that I am taking the piss."

Watching *Neighbours* felt like being at a children's show where they have a whole other subtext for the grown-ups: "Max, you're the birthday boy, would you like to hold my balls while I hide the salami?"

Jump that shark! Jump that shark! Ratings are falling but you still have a massive worldwide audience, so I reckon you should give it the *Chances* treatment, which included man-eating plants, an angel on a motorbike, an Egyptian sun goddess and neo-Nazis.

I want vampires, nympho lesbians, aliens, incest, exorcisms and Toadie on a jet ski actually jumping a shark. Keep up the good work.

Home and Away

You'd think that 1.3 million Australians couldn't be wrong. They can. I know because I've just watched three episodes of *Home and Away*. Remember what I said about *McLeod's Daughters*? Well, multiply that by six-hundred-billion. Forget the War on Terror; it's time for the War on *Home and Away*. The biggest threat to the fibre of our society and the lives of our children is not Osama bin Laden or George Bush; it's this televisual atrocity.

Where do I start? I can finish the line "You know we belong together" with "You and I together forever." How is it possible for me, and you, to know all the words to the *Home and Away* theme song without watching one single episode? I blame the government.

The cast members' level of attractiveness is in inverse proportion to their acting ability. But it's not that these young folk can't act that I find alarming. It's that they can barely string two words together. Through the 67 excruciating minutes I kept feeling as if I was watching a sketch comedy parody of a really bad Australian soap, without the jokes.

The first episode opens with big drama at Summer Bay. Rape? Murder? International espionage? No. Someone has stolen two bottles of Scotch from the surf club. Then it's all, "Shut up, Cassie," "Why would you want to hang around with a lowlife like me?" and "This isn't about Macca any more" [FLICKS HAIR. WALKS OFF. GOES TO BEACH. SITS ON ROCKS. LOOKS ENIGMATIC].

I was extremely distressed that in three episodes I did not once hear Alf Stewart say "flaming mongrels." But he was in a constant state of exasperation, shaking his head and sucking air through his teeth. Irene is the character who really worries me. The rough diamond with a heart of gold speaks fluent Aussie cliché: "Fair dinkum. How anyone could be so stupid considerin' how much grievin' this town has been goin' through is beyond me," and "What the flipping 'eck is goin' on? Are you out of your tiny moind?" Sure we need to hear Australian voices on our screens – but that Australian voice?

It is impossible for *Home and Away* to dumb down the viewers because anyone who watches this show must be brain dead already.

Dickheads by the Sea is Australian content. But that doesn't explain why it is seen in more than 50 countries. It reminds me of that old Billy Crystal gag: Abe walks in to find his best friend Sol having sex with his wife. Abe says, "Sol. I have to. But you?"

Neighbours has produced stars such as Kylie Minogue, Guy Pearce and Russell Crowe. *Home and Away*? Bec Cartwright.

I would rather saw off my children's limbs than let them watch this offensive insult to even the biggest moron. And if you think that I'm being too hard, tune in. But don't blame me if you end up punching a hole in the television or calling Amnesty International to report an abuse of human rights.

60 Minutes

We all have our guilty pleasures. For some it might be eating Milo straight out of the tin, for others it may be indulging in a little wacky tabaccy. I'm not proud of it but watching *60 Minutes* is one of my guilty pleasures. And like my other guilty pleasures (see above), I do it every Sunday night *in the nude.*

My two favourite shows are *Foreign Correspondent* and *Australia's Funniest Home Videos*, so I suppose it makes sense that I enjoy a bit of *60 Minutes* action. It's a kind of hybrid of the two shows: hard-hitting journalism on the one hand and people falling flat on their faces on the other.

Maybe I like it because I wrote one of my first sketches for telly when they were looking for a new reporter back in 1992. It went: [TICKING CLOCK] "I'm Ray Martin. I'm George Negus. I'm Jana Wendt. And I'm Ugly Dave Gray and my wife's so ugly I have to take her to the park on a lead..."

In technical terms, *60 Minutes* is an investigative television news-magazine which revolutionised current affairs with its reporter-centred long-form news stories. In layman's terms, it's crap. High-quality low-rent middle-of-the-road crap. A typical line-up goes something like this:

Tick, tick, tick, tick, tick. On *60 Minutes* tonight: rape and corruption, Tom Hanks plugs his new movie, a four-year-old doctor and something cute about dolphins. Then on to the mailbag: proof that bogans, lunatics and fundamentalists can write.

Now that's a top night in.

I'm fairly sure that *60 Minutes* is not supposed to be taken seriously. Kind of like those fruit wraps. Oh sure, nudge, nudge, wink, wink. Sure, *technically* it's fruit. Sure it's "serious journalism." They include just the right amount of stories about environmental vandalism and Palestine to make you feel as if you are being informed, but the vast majority of the show is puff pieces, tabloid journalism, scaremongering and beat-ups. And how much do the presenters love themselves when they get to do nauseatingly sycophantic celebrity profiles on hacks, has-beens and one-hit wonders? A lot.

60 Minutes does a remarkable job of simplifying some very complex subjects, which is good and bad. Bad because complex things should never be simplified and good because at least it raises awareness about important issues that viewers may usually consider a little "too intellectual 'n' that" for them. It makes you wonder if half-informed is better than un-informed.

Growing up, Sunday night meant a bowl of *Rice-o-Riso* in front of *The Kenny Everett Show, Countdown* and *The Six-Million-Dollar Man* to the sound of my mother gently sobbing on the couch. These days the sound of the ticking of the *60 Minutes* clock means back to work tomorrow for most people. But at my house it means time for mum to take a break from her gentle sobbing to start yelling, "If you kids don't brush your teeth and go to bed I will call the police and they will put you in jail. But bring me the Milo and a spoon first. And the remote control."

A Current Affair

I won't lie to you. I was more excited than John Howard finding a nude picture of Don Bradman in his lunchbox when I sat down to gorge on a few gold-label episodes of *A Current Affair*.

I promised myself three episodes of *ACA* as a reward for putting up with my selfish, foul-mouthed, Little Lord Fauntleroys for the school holidays. On the last day of The Fortnight of Terror, I rewarded myself by locking The Evil Ones in the car, plumping up the cushions, ripping open a block of chocky and luxuriating in the putrid toe-jam of the television world. All to congratulate myself for not donating the little maggots for medical experiments or being approached by *ACA* to appear on the show as the mother of Australia's Most Hideous Children.

To indulge in this expertly produced, finely tuned, exquisite masterpiece of manipulation – and get paid for it – was delicious. Scaremongering? Alarmist conspiracies? Panic inciting? All with the happy ending of a kid with no head getting their wish of meeting Delta Goodrem? You want it? You got it! All hosted by a woman who appears to have a different face every night.

If you watched this show regularly you would never leave your house. You would be so terrified of being infected with a drug-resistant strain of Dodgy Builder from a gang of fat kids who can't read that you'd build a bunker, sew your savings into the roof of your mouth and eat your own flesh.

I don't watch the show. And it's not that I don't want to. Of course I want to. The Neighbours From Hell, Australia's Dirtiest Hooker, the Nursing Home That Makes Pensioners Drink Weed Killer. It is humanly impossible not to get sucked in by the teasers. It's a case of "What are you watching this crap for? Turn it up, will you?"

In the shows I saw I was spewing that there were no reports on the alarming levels of fecal matter on ATM machines, teenage single mothers ripping off Aussie battlers or the footage of our public hospitals that the government didn't want you to see. But I did see the vampire who married her dead zombie boyfriend in a Viking ceremony; the woman attempting to buy a house so she can dig up the bodies of her mother and sister that she is convinced are buried under a concrete slab in the back room; over-zealous parking inspectors; and the breakthrough treatment for beating chronic pain forever.

As I watched people willingly appear on this show I kept reminding myself, "It's OK. They're intelligent adults using mature judgement to make informed decisions." Bullshit. This show preys on the stupid, the naive, the gullible and the ignorant. They wrap it all up and call it television. And 1.2 million people every night encourage them.

This show is an intelligence test. If you tune in, you failed. And if you produce it, you should be jailed in a cell with a 200-kilogram felon who answers to "Princess."

Today Tonight

After watching three episodes of *A Current Affair* last week I was hanging out like a junkie for another fix of low-rent, high-rating tabloid journalism. So I had no choice but to attempt to get a hit by snorting three episodes of *Today Tonight*. And let me tell you, man, that stuff is seriously heavy gear.

When I think of *Today Tonight*, I still can't help thinking of Naomi Robson, even though she was released back into the wild late last year. After watching her report Steve Irwin's death wearing a khaki shirt with a lizard crawling up her arm, Wawa and the cannibals, an out-take that featured the hostess with the mostess swearing seven times in 34 seconds and rumours of make-up vans at Beaconsfield, it was sad tuning in and not seeing her face damning, judging and panicking ordinary Australians, Aussie battlers and suburban mums and dads.

The show hasn't been the same since Naomi left. Although it did come close early this year when the program featured pensioners chained up in nursing homes.

Today Tonight is morbidly fascinating. I can't see one ad without wanting to tune in to the show. If it wasn't so dangerous it would be hilarious. If you compare *TT* with *ACA*, we're talking similar features, longer hair; we're talking same car, different model; we're talking peas and pods. Choosing between the two is a little like choosing which bucket of spew you want to drink.

But people have very clear preferences. "Oh no, *Today Tonight* is beneath me. But that Tracy Grimshaw, now she's very sophisticated."

Each show tries to market itself as The Classy One. But both of them are as classy as flashing a brown eye while wearing a Fletcher Jones skirt.

Anna Coren is glorious to look at. She has a caring energy and an intelligent face. The woman is golden, until she opens her mouth. The pensioner who almost lost her house! Asians are stealing our jobs! The evolutionary slim-suit that can take 5 centimetres off your figure! Epidemic of thievery! Get-rich-quick scheme! Supermarkets ripping you off by up to 300 per cent! And the real-estate agent who is suing the parents of a dead girl for the weeks it took them to find a new tenant after her death.

But the piece that made my jaw drop was the story of Nene King hitting rock bottom. The same Nene King who was once one of Australia's most powerful women and editor of *New Idea*. The teaser featured Nene King looking straight down the barrel saying, "My name is Nene King and I'm a drug addict." Sad, but commercial-television gold.

News and current affairs have always been the battle-ground of Australian commercial television and I bet the networks would love to settle the stoush once and for all with a scrag-fight between the hosties complete with the election-debate worm.

I can't help feeling that these shows would quite happily shoot a disabled child out of a cannon and into the mouth of a waiting child-molester if they thought it would boost the ratings. Which it would.

Border Security

As we all know, I'm not a proper television reviewer, but I did pretend to be the other day by checking out the ratings. As I scanned the national top 20 – *It Takes Two, 60 Minutes, Where Are They Now?*, Seven News – I despaired. But I was, at the same time, a little smug as I thought to myself, "Yes, well that's what the bogans are watching."

(Which reminds me, I received a letter from Joan, of Myrtleford, asking me to explain what a bogan is. So I will. There is a scientific equation to determine precisely whether you, or someone close to you, is a bogan: if your television is wider than your washing machine you are a bogan. The people who live over the road park their television in the driveway between the trailer they use to transport their Rottweilers to dog shows, and the carton of fags their 12-year-old smokes. They are bogans. And the bigger the telly, the bigger the bogan. OK, that's sorted.)

Border Security is the most watched show in Australia, with almost 2 million viewers. Mostly bogan. How do I know? I don't. I'm just guessing. But the bogans over the road are big fans. So I gave it the Deveny Three-Episode Treatment.

THOUSANDS OF MEN AND WOMEN DEDICATE THEIR LIVES TO PROTECTING AUSTRALIA'S BORDER.

Talk about putting the sizzle back into cavity searches.

Thousands of men and women dedicate their lives to protecting Australia's border and after watching three episodes of this documentary/advertisement/propaganda I started thinking, "Who would want to be a jet-setting rock god, a Hollywood megastar or a secret agent of international espionage when you could work in customs?"

Hey, thrill seekers – tried ice climbing, base-jumping and skydiving? Looking for a new rush? This program turns working in the public service into an extreme sport. It's more than, "Did you pack your own bag?" It's fully sick.

Border Security gives the viewer, or in my case, the piss-taker, an opportunity to take a peak under the bonnet of the Australian Customs Service, and it is fascinating. The show pumps the whole business up with a soundtrack heavy on cock-rock, not that it needs any more excitement, it's adrenalised enough.

The show is alarming and comforting at the same time. It's, "Alert! Alert! Funny coloured people who don't speak English being dodgy trying to rip us off blind," on one hand, and then, "But don't worry, the government has it all under control so just sit back, watch *McLeod's Daughters* and relax. We have everything under control." It's cops and robbers. It's good versus evil. It's us and them.

This show should be called *Sprung Bad*. Drugs mules, exotic snakes, illegal workers and a mental case throwing his false teeth at the customs officers when asked to pay the duty on a slab of fags, all sprung bad. The drug dogs are clever, the customs officers are big on hunches and an overly chatty passenger is asking for some personal time with Mr Rubber Glove. Probably safer just to stay home.

The Footy Show

I have just watched three episodes of *The Footy Show* and I feel like Sammy Davis Jnr at a Ku Klux Klan rally, like Dannii Minogue at a Mensa convention, like George Pell in 2007.

I'm not into plants but I like *Gardening Australia*, I'm not into quiz shows but I like *The Einstein Factor*, I'm not into cars but I like *Top Gear*, so not being into footy isn't the reason that I'm repelled by this destructive, small-minded, morally bankrupt orgy of chauvinism. *The Footy Show* is a celebration of the very worst that television, sport, Australia and human beings can cook up. It's offensive, toxic and corrosive. It encourages viewers to be stupid, shallow and sexist. Sit down, shut up and hang on. And ladies, bring a plate.

The Footy Show is nothing more than media-sanctioned misogyny. And so much less. Tune in and you'll feel you've woken up in 1952. A man in a full-body condom, men dressed as women, girls in bikinis, guys stuffing toilet paper down their jocks, dickheads, wankers and yobs. The few women that I did see were leered at, one called "a bitch" and another told to "get fucked" (both by Sam Newman). I heard the word "sheilas" and could sense that the words "poofters," "wogs," "slopes" and "spastics" were just below the surface.

Is it the program, the network, the culture of Australian television or just Newman that is so offensive? It's all of them. But Newman really needs to be singled out for his extraordinary contribution to this tragic, puerile, adolescent show that degrades the culture of football, alienates women and teaches boys that females are slaves, trophies or bitches.

No wonder young footballers are taking drugs. How else can they reconcile this bizarre world with real life? And what's with the suits? Some pathetic attempt to bring respectability to this sad little show? Fat chance.

Newman is vain, ugly, a megalomaniac, a bully. I can't help feeling that deep inside he would be happy for women to have their brains removed and replaced with bar fridges. He's a dangerous bloke who's paid a lot of money to defile our culture and undermine our intelligence in the most putrid fashion. For any of you who have sat surrounded by people laughing at this maggot and found yourself thinking there is something wrong with you, there isn't. There's something wrong with him. And them.

The Footy Show catapults sexism into an extreme sport. Football shows don't have to be a cross between a buck's night and a lynching. And if you don't believe me, watch *Before the Game*. It's not as blokey, and that's not just because there is a woman on the panel but because the blokes are not as blokey. The jokes are not as blokey. And the content is intelligent. Think Roy and H.G., *Live and Sweaty*, *Talking Footy* and *The Fat*. Australia has an impressive history and culture of intelligent, entertaining sports shows that put *The Footy Show* to shame.

Talking points

Clipboards

It's that time of year when parents begin wringing their sweaty palms about where their kinder child should start school next year. I laughed like a drain when I heard reports of parents at primary school open-days with clipboards. I didn't believe it, of course, until a mate told me that several of her mothers' group were guilty as charged.

"With clipboards?" "Yes, with clipboards." "To check out a school?" "No, to check out about six schools." At this point I fell off my chair in hysterics. "So tell me, what are these mothers trying to find in a school?" "Well, Dev, they are trying to find the school that is going to turn their child into a genius." BINGO. So if they can't be a genius maybe their kid can be the genius they might have been. Now that sounds like healthy parenting. Why would anyone want their kid to be a genius? I just want my kids to be well-rounded, resilient and not in jail. All I hope is that by the time they are 25 they have survived a broken heart, a flat tyre, food poisoning and have a couple of good mates. Bad mother, me.

When our eldest started school, I met a woman at the school information night. She listed off eight primary schools that she had already checked out. I said: "We're only seeing this one." By the grave look on her face it was as if the principal was Pol Pot and the teachers were ex-military personnel from Abu Ghraib. "Forgot to do your homework? Stay in after school and form a naked human pyramid with the kids from the special-needs class."

I'd love to tell you that I turned to her and said: "Get over yourself, you insecure wanker." But I didn't. All we wanted was for our son to turn up on the first day of school and know a familiar face from kinder. Because you can't tell if a place is right for your kid simply by wandering around the corridors.

Here's a tip. If you have checked out more than two schools it's probably a good idea to consider getting yourself a life at some stage. If you have a good reason not to send them to the local primary school, send them to the next closest. If you feel the difference is between a child who will be a Nobel Prize-winner and a child who is a crack-addicted hooker, you're wrong.

Here's a message from all of us here at Calm Down International: "If you are so tragic that you need your kids to go to a certain school to feel better about yourself may I suggest that you take a short course, do some volunteer work or try yoga."

What is best for kids is not the idyllic school environment as perceived by their anxious, hovering parents. Children are better equipped for life by learning persistence and motivation through failure, disappointment and frustration than by some fantasy school created by their parents' inner five-year-old. Kids just want: a place to play chasey, some teachers who know their name and a few mates they can laugh and swap lunches with.

Most kids don't give a rat's about the improvised music workshops, organic gardens and interpretative-dance classes they do at school. But the parents, eyes blazing, face alight, will bore you senseless about them in an attempt to convince you of their coolness. All it actually does is convince us that they are Wannabe Creatives; insecure dags who had friends in bands but were never in bands themselves. Too much exposure to organised creativity immunises children against creativity. I can guarantee you that they will never hunger to paint like Monet, read Shakespeare or play cello like Casals because: "Nah. I did that when I was six and I was crap at it. Let's go to the casino!"

As far as holding them back for an extra year: when in doubt, hold them back. If kinder has suggested that they can do with another year, hold them back. If you are thinking that the earlier you get a child into school the more you can stuff into them, hold them back. If these instructions from me are pissing you off because people around you are suggesting that you hold your kid back, hold them back. I do not know of one parent who has held a child back and regretted it, but I know dozens of parents who sent them early who do. If your defence is that they'll be bored at home, trust me: kids are always bored at home.

There have been countless studies showing that starting children early may have academic, social and psychological disadvantages, but it's simply common sense to have kids coping as best as possible in the classroom rather than struggling, or worse still, being held back. It's an individual decision and the government desperately needs to increase funding to kindergartens and establish more preschool programs for four-to-five-year-olds attached to schools to make this decision easier.

Private Education I

I've wanted to write about the social apartheid and false economy of private schools for a while. And the government's "privatisation by stealth" of the education system. So a few months ago I hunted down the speech that writer Shane Maloney made to Scotch College. Reading it, I cheered, thumped the table and yelled "hallelujah" at the sheer brilliance and balls of Maloney. I then slumped in a heap thinking, "Well, there's no point me writing anything because he's said everything that I want to, but much better."

A recent chance meeting with Maloney had me gushing about the speech and explaining my quandary. He encouraged me to basically "just say it all again." So Shane Maloney, if you're out there, this one's for you. And for the 70 per cent of parents who send their children to government schools. And for the 70 per cent of students who attend them.

Here's something in the budget that you may have missed: Federal funding for private schools will increase from $5.8 billion to $7.5 billion over the next five years. Funding to public schools will rise from $3.1 billion to $3.4 billion over the next five years. Shame on us.

Here's where I stand: private schools should not receive funding. That's it. We have a police force funded by the government. If you want a bodyguard or private security, you pay for it out of your own pocket.

The same should go for schools. If you want your child to go to a school where they wear blazers so you can get over your own insecurities, or the chip on your own shoulder, you should pay for it. Every single cent.

And it should be compulsory for all politicians to send their children to government schools. And use only public healthcare.

It's liberating not to be worried about where my young sons will be going to high school. It will be one of the closest government high schools. If things don't work out, we'll try somewhere else. It's not their education. It's their school. Not the same thing. The school a child attends has no bearing on their future success or happiness. I'm disgusted by parents' nauseating obsession with the perfect school for their perfect child. Parents panic that any "wrong" decision may mess up their kid's potential trajectory. They seem to believe that kids can simply be programmed by their parents' desires. Here's a tip: instead of both working full-time just so you can send your kids to a private school, cut down your work, be less stressed, stop outsourcing your life, send them to the local secondary and be home more. Teenagers need, and want, their parents to be around.

Sending children to private schools seems to be less about parents doing what they think is best for their child and more a case of parents wanting their children to have something better than every other child. Education is the entire community's responsibility and the outcome affects us all.

I am torn between saying that public schools desperately need more funding and writing about how wonderful they are. Both of which are true. The lessons kids learn in government schools – resilience, motivation, community and tolerance – hold them in much better stead than hand-holding, spoon-feeding, mollycoddling and segregation.

When I think of kids less fortunate than my own, I think of kids stuck in middle-class, single-sex white ghettos from the age of five (or four if they're "gifted").

The independent and Christian schools are divisive, discriminatory, reliant on hand-outs and implicitly teach children that some kids deserve nicer playgrounds than others. Even within their own tribe. The preps at Burke Hall surely don't deserve better facilities than the preps at St Gabriel's in Reservoir. Give me a child when they are seven and I'll show you an invoice for $12,477 (excluding uniforms, excursions and music lessons) for something they could get around the corner for free.

I added up what it would cost to send my three children to a middle-of-the-range private school for six years. Not counting uniforms, excursions, transport, building funds etc. And it was about $330,000, give or take. My first thought? No one can be getting value for money. My second thought? I could buy my kids a degree for that amount of money, and I might have to if education keeps heading the way it is. But I'm hoping that my kids will all be tradies. Because the happiest blokes I know are the tradies. People say, "Stop funding private schools? It's not as easy as that."

Yes it is. Like smoking in hospitals, gender-based pay and taking babies away from unmarried mothers, funding private education is something we will look back on and be ashamed of.

Private Education II

I met this bloke at a party a while back. He had been teaching at private schools for many years. "Lifelong learning," "independent thinkers," "creative minds." "That's what the brochures say, but it's all bullshit," he spat, "The motto for our school should be: 'open wide.'"

"So what do your kids think of the school?" I asked, referring to his students. He misunderstood.

"My kids? I wouldn't send my kids there if you paid me. They go to the local secondary school. I wouldn't want my kids to think that was real life. They'd never learn anything."

So why did he work there? "Better conditions. Better

resources. It's easier to teach." He told me that he'd recently started applying for jobs in the government system because "private schools are businesses."

Private-school teachers shouldn't have to choose to work within a system that they have political and ethical reservations about simply so they can get the most out of their careers. If the government stopped sucking-up to the private schools, they wouldn't have to. I don't blame people wanting to enjoy their work. I want teachers to love what they do. I just want them to be able to do it in a comprehensive, generously funded, well-resourced government school system.

Steven Levitt's book *Freakonomics* is a ripper read. The maverick economist quotes studies that prove IQ is strongly hereditary and suggests that children should choose their parents wisely. He found the only factors that made any impact on kids' academic-test scores were "things that parents are" not "things that parents do."

"Parents who are well-educated, successful and healthy tend to have children who test well in school; but it doesn't seem to matter much whether a child is trotted off to museums or spanked … frequently read-to or plopped in front of the television."

Levitt highlights a fascinating finding in the Chicago school system. In 1980, Chicago attempted to desegregate its schools by allowing children to attend any school they wished. If too many students applied for any one school, a lottery was held. Whether the student got into the "better school" or not made no impact on the students' educational outcome. But the fact that they participated in the lottery did. In other words, it was not the outcome of the lottery that mattered, but the students' participation, which was an indication of their desire to do well. So if you want your children to go to the best school possible, send them to the local and save the money.

How hilarious yet quite tragic it is to hear adults refer to other adults as "Scotch boys," "Carey girls," "St Kevin's boys" or "Geelong Grammar girls." This all tends to stop when they discover that I went to Reservoir High. People tell me that private schools give their children the opportunity to meet "the right people" (which makes the 70 per cent-plus of us who attended government schools the "wrong" people). And that they "make good connections" and "do valuable networking." Do parents have no faith in their children? I want my children to succeed on ability, persistence and merit. Not on some bizarre, anachronistic club that your parents pay for you to join.

The Labor Party's rhetoric about supporting parents' rights to choose is simply pork-barrelling to keep the aspirationals and the churches onside. How can they say that they are committed to "fund all schools on the basis of need and fairness" and then say, "we will not cut funding to any school"?

Many gifted teachers have left the teaching profession. And many potential teachers will never stand in front of a classroom thanks to low pay, poor conditions and limitations on their own initiative. If you want the best teachers possible, the answer is cheap and effective. Pay teachers $100,000 a year, minimum. It's the long way round but the short way home. The long-term benefits mean this overdue wage correction saves the community billions in the long term.

Our school had a fete recently and a staggering number of parents put in hundreds of hours to raise the equivalent of 12 months' private-school tuition for one child. But the sense of community was magic. I can't help wondering why it is that the defence force, the Australian Institute of Sport and the parliamentary super fund never have to run lamington drives to raise money.

You can cook up all the "realising our potential," "schools of the future," "education revolution" sizzle you like, but it is a mark of a civilised society to have free high-quality schools. Why can't we set an example to the rest of the world? Oh, I know. Because that would require leadership, commitment, courage and vision. And involve us overcoming our insecurity about being a provincial backwater.

Smacking

The Australian Childhood Foundation has launched a campaign to warn parents not to smack their children because it may "teach children that violence can be an acceptable way to solve problems." A recent poll revealed that 92 per cent thought that smacking was "sometimes" necessary.

I've never been sucked in by any of the fads and fashions in the extreme sport of parenting. I'm such a maverick mother my kids were all on solid food at three months. Which is why I can't believe that I'm agreeing with something called the Australian Childhood Foundation.

Don't get me wrong, my kids annoy me as much as the next person's do. But I don't hit them. I have never hit them and will never hit them. There have been moments when I have thought, "Ah, this is when parents hit." But I haven't. Because they are children and I am an adult. I pick on people my own size.

I'm not the perfect parent. Ask my kids. I give the three kids two Freddo frogs and tell them to fight it out between them. Every night I kiss them goodnight and whisper to each of them, "You're not my favourite, but you're getting pretty close." I often respond to the question "why can't you take us to the park?" with "because I hate children, I hate the park and I am flat-out reading *New Weekly*."

There's a book called *The Good Enough Parent*. I've never read it but the title sums up my attitude completely. I'm not a helicopter parent, constantly hovering; I'm a bad-luck-you'll-live-get-over-it parent.

But despite my "can't be stuffed" attitude, I wouldn't kick a kitten, so why would I hit a kid? I love the response, "It didn't do me any harm." Well, yes, it did, because you are now inflicting violence on children instead of seeing it as abuse. Smacking kids is wrong. End of story. Violence or the threat of violence is an abuse of the responsibility we have as parents and as humans.

I can understand someone having a knee-jerk reaction if a toddler bites them unexpectedly. I can even understand someone doing it because they never knew how far they would be pushed. Once. But beyond that it's just bullying and exploiting your physical advantage.

Parents who smack for the first time are racked with guilt. Then time passes, their kid isn't in therapy, they start using smacking as a threat and before you know it, it is normalised and often joked about in lighter moments: "Oh, you watch out or I'll paddle your cute little bottom." But when they do, there's nothing cute about it. I have been sickened listening to countless people recount hitting their children. They have a sadistic smile and a glint in their eyes.

"It's not a smack really, it's just a tap." Then why bother?

What, so just a little bit of violence is OK? Well probably a couple of cigarettes won't hurt them either.

The smackers say that smacking doesn't work. They tell me that they hit because they are stressed out and at the end of their tether. "So why wouldn't you smack an adult?" "Because they're big and will hit back." Some parents have told me that smacking makes them feel better. Here's a tip, try meditation, a facial or self-control.

Put the kids in a room and tell them that you are angry but you are coming back. Punch the wall, have a drink, phone a friend or yell if you like. Why is yelling better than smacking? Because you are much bigger than them. If the yelling escalates, it's still just yelling. If the violence escalates, they don't know that you are not going to kill them.

It's not just "a little smack," it's physical violence. Why are children not protected in the same way as adults? An adult hitting another is considered assault, but an adult hitting a child is considered reasonable parenting.

When is old enough? Six months? Where is the line between smacking and child abuse? Why is it only OK to hit them if you love them? Why, in domestic violence situations, is there a zero-tolerance policy but it's OK if you hit, slap, punch, kick, pinch or shove a kid as long as you don't leave a mark?

I could back in a whole lot of statistics, but what would be the point? Hits from the '60s, '70s, '80s and today. Wrong, wrong, wrong. All wrong.

Before we had children, my partner and I (who had both been hit as children) made the choice not to smack. Which is the only reason that schools no longer beat, strap and whip kids. A conscious decision.

Smacking children diminishes us all. It's time to break

the cycle with some re-education, realistic alternatives and some shaming.

If you are proud of hitting your kids, hit 'em harder and hit 'em in front of other people. That'll prove me wrong.

Private Health Insurance

How can anyone not agree with free, universal high-quality healthcare? How can anyone think that our current public–private marriage of political convenience is beneficial to all Australians both now and in the future? How can anyone think that our nation is getting value for money? It's not.

Private health insurance is a rip-off. Public health needs the $3-billion government subsidy that is propping-up the private health insurance industry. And a truck-load more. People don't need a 30 per cent rebate on their private health insurance premiums. They need not to feel terrified into having to pay the premiums in the first place.

My solution? Make it mandatory for politicians and their families to use only the public health system.

Government subsidy of private health is theft from the public health system. It's a disgrace. Where is the choice if you are on benefits or a low income and you can't afford private health insurance? "Chicken or beef, sir?" That's a choice.

Having private health insurance is not a choice. The poor, the old and the vulnerable wait in pain. The rest get served first. Why is pain and loss of quality of life not as important if the person is old, poor or on benefits? It's discrimination. It's an economically-adjusted pain scale. "They're doing it tough so a bit more pain won't hurt 'em."

Last week I found myself on the Medi-Go-Round. It was one of those "it's probably nothing, it's probably nothing, it's probably nothing, maybe it's cancer" scenarios. After six months of niggles that had grown to excruciating discomfort, I was off to the doctor. There was talk of having something removed. I don't have private health insurance. I've never had it. I'm politically and philosophically opposed to it.

But I also have the courage of my convictions to tell you that if I were facing six months on a waiting list or six months of misery, I would be happy to pay out of my own pocket and jump the queue. It's not fair that I can do that. I want my taxes used efficiently, or to pay more tax so that we can all be treated in order of need and not of wealth.

Start talking to people about why they have private health insurance and you'll realise that hospital waiting lists are the best advertisement and incentive for private health insurance there is. The government has no interest in reducing the waiting lists because the waiting lists are saving them money that they can spend on important things, such as the parliamentary super fund, $9000-a-roll silk wallpaper for the Prime Minister's plane and more defence toys and war bling.

People will tell you that they have private health insurance because they were sucked in by the fear of waiting lists, getting into "the breeding zone," the 2000 run-for-cover campaign or simply "because my accountant told me to." None of them will tell you that they think it's value for money. Most of them are opposed to it. Necessary evil. They will tell you that they don't notice the payments and that any rebate feels like a bonus.

If negative optimism is "it won't happen to me," then

positive optimism must be "maybe it will." Once people sign up to private health insurance they are reluctant to pull out because: "What if I get hit by a car tomorrow?" And for the people who convince themselves that having private health insurance is taking pressure off public hospitals, it's not. It's making the situation worse.

It's clever how the government is taking away with one hand and giving back with the other. "Oh, look at what a mess the public health system is in! Whoever did that should be smacked. And look at the Medicare levy surcharge. Outrageous! Here's a rebate on your private health insurance and a lovely safety net. What did you say? A safety net will only encourage the increase of fees and not benefit the public in any way, shape or form? Don't be so cynical. We're your government and we love you." It's all smoke and mirrors, ladies and gentlemen.

I pay the Medicare levy surcharge and I want it to go to Medicare. At present, it doesn't. It probably goes to pay for John Howard's nose-hair clippers, or some more taxpayer-funded government advertising.

Tomorrow, Michael Moore's documentary about the US health system, *Sicko*, opens in cinemas around Australia. When you watch this movie, think of it as "here's one we prepared earlier."

There is a proverb: "A society grows great when old men plant trees whose shade they know they shall never sit in." With free high-quality universal healthcare there will be shade for our children. With the increase of private health there will be no shade because there will be no trees.

I love a good rant. I feel better now.

Consumerism

Reduce greed. There's your answer. Thank you and good night.

Nothing new, nothing fancy, nothing even slightly original. Here's a tip to increase your happiness. Just stop trying to fill that gaping hole inside yourself with more stuff. Or shelving for the stuff. Or a bigger house for the shelving. It doesn't work. It just makes the hole bigger. Everything won't be fine if you just get new light fittings, replace the curtains or buy a new mobile phone. No one needs 12 doona covers. Everything will be fine if you take a big breath and stop buying crap you don't need with money you don't have to impress people you don't like.

Does anyone else want to slap half the people around you and say "You'd have more peace if you just spent less money"? People complain about how hard they work, how little money they have and how their relationship is at breaking point. And then what do they do? Exercise? Meditate? Work less? Nope. They buy themselves a cappuccino machine they'll only use twice, an exercise bike that will be the most expensive clothes hanger they have ever owned, shoes they'll never wear and then sign up for cable TV. And then put their hand up for more overtime.

Next time you find yourself itching for some retail therapy, think about what would really turn off that desire button inside you, not just put it on snooze. Take a look at your wardrobe overflowing with clothes you don't wear, your shed chockers with tools you don't use or that entertainment unit groaning under the weight of the hundreds of dollars of DVDs and CDs that you've never played. Remember how excited you were and how you truly believed, deep down in the soul of your being, that each purchase would bring you happiness. How it would soothe those wounds of feeling unloved, unappreciated and unhappy. How you had to have it. The thrill of the purchase, the excitement of the homecoming and then the punch in the stomach when your credit-card bill arrived.

Middle-class whingers complaining about how hard they are struggling need a good slap. They are offensive to true battlers out there who stock up on their brand of margarine when it's on special and don't buy new socks but mend the ones they have.

Someone handed me $300 cash the other day. It felt like a million dollars. It felt like far more money than ten times as much sitting in my bank account. Because I could see it, feel it, smell it. These days money is invisible. People don't actually know how much things cost them. If people had to slave away and earn the cash before they could acquire the things they wanted, given the choice and knowing how much sweat it'd taken, they'd go for the cash. The invisible money culture is not only ravaging the environment, it's corroding lives and destroying happiness. Putting it on the credit card or taking money out of the mortgage? It's all invisible money.

I call it the Veruca Salt syndrome. I want it and I want it NOW. People have to have the big house, the new car, the new kitchen, the new clothes NOW. Once upon a time people saved, they waited, they went without. Same happy. Some say more happy.

The symptoms of affluenza, luxury fever and conspicuous consumption can all be alleviated by the simple mantra "I have enough." The worried well need less, not more. The stressed-out full-timers who live on Mortgagee Mountain, between Default District and Foreclosure Falls, dig themselves in deeper as they attempt to find peace in the purchase of plasma TVs so that each member of the family can watch *Big Brother* in their own room of the McMansion.

People are in debt up to their eyebrows and they tell me it's good for the economy. But it's destroying our spiritual economy. Is this the spiritual recession we had to have? Kids want to lie on the grass watching the clouds roll by with chilled-out parents. Not be dragged through shopping centres by harassed mums and dads trying to anaesthetise their existential pain by purchasing more stuff to plug in and more stuff to store.

On any perfect 25-degree windless Sunday you will find Chadstone, Northland, DFO and all those soul-destroying cathedrals of emptiness chockers with people attempting to sedate. Take two transactions and call me in the morning. They'd be better off spending a few hours sitting in a church. And that's coming from an atheist. Greed and consumption addict people and they spend weekends trawling shopping centres chasing the next hit.

Happy is the man who is content with what he has. And the woman who needs only one pair of good shoes and a library card. Maybe I should follow the advice of the graffiti I read last week: SHUT UP AND SHOP.

Baby Boomers

I like baby boomers. I'm not sucking up. I actually do like them. Not all of them. They weren't all a Germaine Greer, a Richard Branson or a John Lennon in their day. Some of them were uptight stiffs who were anti-abortion, pro-war, racist, sexist, homophobic conservatives. And still are with their "that's not music, that's just noise," "a woman's place is in the kitchen" and "gay people need to be cured."

Those social freaks should be put into some kind of Sovereign Hill for anachronisms called The People the '60s Forgot. Detain asylum seekers? Nah. Detain narrow-minded, short-sighted bigots I say. But I would say that, wouldn't I?

I'm deeply grateful to the boomers who did embrace social change: who burnt their bras, grew their hair, bought the Kama Sutra and ate dhal. We gen-Xers, in particular, have directly benefited enormously from their contribution to positive social change, increased awareness, greater acceptance and a broader definition of what's "normal." But society isn't "finished" by any means.

I don't believe that baby boomers should be seen on commercials about life insurance and not heard. But it is time they started bowing out of public life so that the young ones can start setting the agenda and making a more significant contribution to public debate. The boomers have had a fair go and now it's time to invoke the "every kid gets a kick of the footy" rule. Boomers will tell you: "Howard's too old, he should give Costello a turn at being head boy." But they're a bit touchy when you start suggesting that it may be time for their intellectuals and cultural commentators to pack it in and hand over the car keys.

The boomers' contribution needs to be diluted so that new voices and ideas can develop for our society to keep up with itself. I don't want to send all the boomers off on a Probus outing forever, never to be seen again. But it is time they took their rightful place as wise elders dispensing their pearls of wisdom selectively. And for the rest of us to consider the relevance of their suggestions and debate them vigorously. It's unnatural and unhealthy for the movers and shakers of a society to be the same movers and shakers as 30 or 40 years ago.

There'll never be a generation who'll see as much social change in their lifetime as the boomers. What 70-year-old would have believed that their child, their sibling or themselves could be openly gay, have children out of wedlock or be divorced and it not be social suicide? And who would have believed that Aussie kids would have rice crackers with seaweed, spanakopita and hummus in their lunch boxes? Society has undergone almost hydroponic growth in the past 45 years.

Gen-Xers are experiencing a revolution in technological and work culture in our lifetimes as phenomenal as the social revolution the boomers experienced in theirs. The idea of a lifetime with one job, in one organisation, ending with a gold-watch retirement at 65, is a concept our children will consider as far-fetched as we consider lower wages for women.

Coming to terms with social, economic and cultural change is one thing. Wrestling the Great Australian Dream from our psyche will be a nightmare. Boomers: leave some houses for the rest of us. Shouldn't everyone get firsts before people have seconds? Or thirds? Maybe there should be a 5 per cent surcharge to go to public housing or to a first-home-owners' grant fund every time a rental property is purchased. I understand why people invest in houses over share portfolios. We understand houses. We can see them and touch them. The sharemarket? Who knows? Unless of course you actually do. Sure, you may get more return from shares, but you can live in a house. You can't live under a manila folder of share certificates.

That's the problem. There is a sense of security about having a home that is hardwired into us. And renters can just get turfed-out when the landlord's daughter comes back from overseas or when his son gets married. The brave new world predicts that our children will be more likely to own a unicorn than their own home. Is this bad? Or is this just reality and we need to get over it?

Property investment is not the only reason people are finding it difficult to buy a home. There are more of us wanting to buy homes, and more people wanting more in the homes that they buy. The government needs to pull its finger out and provide more public housing so that renters will not all be at the mercy of the landlords and we can all live happily ever after. Even if we are renting.

Gay Marriage

I'm not sure if it's true, but the story goes that when the announcement of the first gay marriage was made on 1 October 1989, one of the editors at this newspaper said, "I've got the headline. With This Ring ..."

Go on. Laugh. It's funny. OK. Gay marriage. I'm strapped in and I'm all ears. Let her rip. Can you explain that to me, please? Same-sex couples have had the guts to follow their hearts and their genitals, to defy "convention" and stereotypes and live boldly, freely, proudly and authentically. They have stood tall, gay and rebellious despite the wrath and the disdain of the uptight white honkies, the religious fundamentalists, the idiots, the conservatives and the right-wing political extremists. So why on earth would they want to get married?

Sure, they should be able to get married – but why would they want to? Why would these glorious public unions that have said "stuff you, this is who I am, like it or join the Young Liberals" buy into an institution that has regarded their love as everything from wrong to degenerate to evil? Why would they want to buy into this antiquated system? This is an institution historically based on inequality, racism, ownership of human beings and sexual and financial control of women and children. Then reinforced by romantic notions fed and fuelled by marketing and the media.

Even the straights are walking away from marriage in droves. You reckon the 7.15 from Dandenong to Flinders Street is chockers? You should check out the 8.05 from Outmoded Expectations to Living In Sin.

Gays, lesbians, queers and homosexuals should be able to get married if that's what turns them on. But they should not have to purely in order for their relationships to be legally ratified for the purposes of superannuation, pensions, taxation and the parenting of their own children. It makes me ashamed to live in a society that denies this fundamental right to human beings.

Gay people don't need to be accepted by this institution that will never fully embrace them. Fuck 'em. Do your own thing. Don't be like us boring old straights and child-obsessed breeders. I saw a postcard the other day. It had an image of a 1950s bride with the words: "Why do I have to get married? I didn't do anything wrong."

That is why the movement by the Melbourne City Council to set up a Relationships Declaration Register is a move in the right direction. Registering a same-sex relationship will not give them the same rights as married couples, but this documented evidence could help in legal proceedings involving inheritances and the division of property. One small step for man-love and woman-love. One giant step for us all.

If same-sex marriage becomes the norm, perhaps it will dilute and loosen-up this dinosaur of a convention. It may force it to evolve into a modern, tolerant and less exclusive legalisation and into a celebration of a union. Maybe this is just what the institution of marriage needs to bring it into the 21st century: some poofs and dykes. But I don't think so. Marriage is a car up on blocks in the front yard. Divorce is thriving.

I can't help feeling that the idea of same-sex marriage conflicts with a fundamental characteristic of being queer. Don't queers pride themselves on being radical, an "other," a tribe that has always stood side by side with subversion?

Yes and no. In the same way that there are many ways of being straight, there are also many ways of being gay, and many ways to be married. Not all marriages involve the woman and offspring taking the husband's name, pronouncing the happy couple "man and wife" or "giving away" the woman by her father (who, by extension, obviously owns her). But an alarming number still do.

Gay marriages, female priests, voluntary euthanasia and hydrogen cars will all eventually become things that we take for granted. In the same way that now we take for granted equal pay for women, the indigenous right to vote and the right for men to cry like babies, push prams and have long hair.

Have a party. Celebrate what you have achieved. Friends of mine, together for 12 years with two children, recently married. Now to me this made more sense; to have a party to celebrate making it this far. I never wonder why people split up; I wonder how they stay together.

Save the money and go to New York for a month, send it to the Asylum Seekers' Resource Centre or get your kitchen done. Or use it for a decadent weekend of rum, sodomy and the lash. Get married if you want. But you don't have to do that for me to celebrate, support and consider your relationship as worthy and equal.

Fast Cars

How about that Grand Prix, eh? One look at the racing fans is all it takes for me to realise that some suburbs should have fences around them. Knuckle-dragging petrol-heads, anorexic bottle-blondes marinated in fake tan and middle-aged blokes with man boobs and pimples on their arses paying exorbitant amounts of money to watch cars go fast. What a disgrace. It's no wonder I drink.

I'm sure the parents of terminally ill children suffering rare diseases for which there is no research funding will take comfort in the fact that the state government has probably spent $30 million on loud, polluting cars while their child dies a painful lonely death in a pool of their own vomit. They'll be at peace as they hold their dear little angel's hand as they slip away knowing that Bernie Ecclestone has pocketed a $20 million licensing fee. There goes my chance of ever being a grid girl.

Don't start banging on about all the revenue that it supposedly (and I stress the word supposedly) creates. You could get a far better long-term return by putting that money into science, education or health.

Why is it that many of the flag-wavers, who are the keenest to use these events to "show off" our home town to tourists, are the ones least willing to share it? If you need to have a Grand Prix looting, marauding and corroding our town to feel "proud," please kill yourself at your earliest possible convenience. And take your "I'm Another Australian Against Further Immigration" T-shirt with you.

It's festival fever here in our beautiful Melbourne and I am part of the festivities in my role hosting the Sydney Road Bakery Tours as part of the Melbourne Food and Wine Festival.

This is not a thinly veiled or heavy-handed plug because this alleged left-wing rag sponsors this festival of feeding. Don't call, they're booked out.

Last week and again this week, I'll show folks around Sydney Road and take them into a handful of the many Middle Eastern bakeries along this lively and cosmopolitan strip of bridal boutiques, multicultural food, funky cafés, factory outlets and rampant tolerance.

It's a gift to take the Loafers into a bakery owned by Iraqis and, after they have met the hard-working and generous couple and their sweet, well-mannered children, and eaten their delicious food, to tell them that these people are asylum seekers from Iraq. The same people that John Howard is leaving stranded on boats or letting rot on Pacific islands.

At our next stop, I introduce them to Houssam with the twinkling eyes, beaming smile and Osama bin Laden beard. He displays kindness, hospitality and warmth and also cooks Lebanese pastries so delicious they bring tears to your eyes. Let's hope it dilutes the widely held belief that all Lebanese men are rapists.

Next stop is Jenny the Turkish mother of five who makes gozleme (stuffed pastries). She arrived from Turkey 37 years ago, first landing in the Northern Territory. The blackfellas told her that they ate white people (this had her terrified for weeks) and then taught her English, "bad words first."

"I feel like I am in another country," the wide-eyed Loafers say as they openly gawk at the young girls wearing the hijab and tight jeans SMSing and drinking Coke. It should be called the Meet Your First Muslim tour. Don't be alert, don't be alarmed, shake their hands, eat their food and enjoy the hospitality they extend. Marvel at the warmth they radiate despite (or possibly because of) the horrors they have seen and the hours they spend building a better life in what they hope is a decent and tolerant society.

My favourite moment of each tour is as we cross Sydney Road and I hold up a stick with a loaf of bread on it and stop the traffic. Not just any traffic, but; I tell them all to look out for a four-wheel drive. As the four-wheel drive approaches, I walk onto the road and hold up my stick, ushering the Loafers across with the words: "Sorry, this is an emergency. These people have not eaten for three minutes. You are not a local, please take the next right, which will take you to South Yarra."

One of the Loafers said: "I'm from Brighton, dear, and if you did that where I'm from, you'd be run down."

"Yes," I replied. "That's why I live here."

Unless you need to tow a horse float or you are the Bush Tucker Man, you don't need a four-wheel drive. When I walk along High Street, Malvern, and see rows of four-wheel-drives that have spent even less time in the bush than Telstra, I want to pull out my key and scratch into their pristine duco: BUY A SMALLER CAR YOU GREEDY

SELFISH FUCK. Or: RIDE A BIKE AND SAVE ON THE LIPO.

Give me pide, gozleme and baklava, not circuses.

Big Cars

I would like to sincerely apologise for the comments I made about four-wheel drives in last week's column.

Due to a limitation on the number of words, I was unable to say everything I wanted about these dangerous and obnoxious monster-trucks being driven by people selfish at best and ignorant at worst.

And not just shame on you for driving these anti-social, arrogant four-wheeled bullies. Shame on the car companies for appealing to your insecurity by sucking you in with slogans like "Give way – not" (Jeep), "Get in or get out of the way" (Toyota HiLux) or the "class-kicking" HiLux four-wheel-drive utility with its "intimidating styling," "aggressive bonnet scoop" and "dominating moulded front bumpers." YEAH! What next? "Kill everyone and destroy the planet NOW WITH FREE AIR!" Suck up that free air, baby, because soon we'll be paying for it.

When I discovered that the word Pajero really is Spanish for wanker, I thought to myself: "It must be my birthday!"

And just so we are clear, bush folk, people towing horse floats and the like, you're off the hook. I'm talking about the people driving tanks to do the shopping and drop their kids off at school.

I can't be fagged unpacking the arrogance of the space they take up on the road, which is the equivalent of taking up eight seats at the cinema and wearing a refrigerator as a hat. And I'm not going to get into their environmental impact, as there must be at least one four-wheel drive that is greener than the lowered Commodores with mags that fang down my street blowing blue smoke. But you'd have to be an idiot not to put together the basic larger-vehicle-equals-more-fuel-necessary-particularly-on-city-roads equation.

Need the space? Try a station wagon, roof racks or a little inconvenience. So your kids have long legs? Where are these kids with the two-metre legs? The only place I've ever seen them is in the Moomba parade, and I thought they were actually normal-sized people on stilts.

So let's get this party started and crack open an icy-cold can of facts, shall we? Let's slip into something a little more uncomfortable with the four-wheel drive safety myth.

Research conducted by the Monash University Accident Research Centre has concluded that four-wheel drives are almost twice as likely to roll than a car, resulting in their drivers being 3.4 times more likely to be killed due to crushed cabin space.

The centre has pointed out that four-wheel drives "are not subject to the full range of design rules applicable to passenger cars and their derivatives."

A team from Imperial College London and the University of Queensland found, after a study of more than 40,000 vehicles, that "four-wheel drive drivers were almost four times more likely than car drivers to be using a mobile phone and 26 per cent more likely not to wear a seatbelt." The researchers concluded that four-wheel drive owners take more risks because they feel safer.

The Australian Transport Safety Bureau found that half the 36 children killed in driveway deaths between 1996 and 1998 were struck by large four-wheel drives. They have also found: "The proportion of alcohol intoxication amongst four-wheel drive drivers involved in fatal crashes (29 per cent) was higher than for all other types of vehicle." And: "In four-wheel drive crashes involving multiple vehicles, passenger car occupants accounted for the largest proportion of fatalities (64 per cent). Four-wheel drive occupants accounted for 18 per cent."

Children are at risk because they are little and these vehicles are high. As far as proximity sensors are concerned, they do bugger all to protect children. According to NRMA Insurance's Robert McDonald, "they only work about a metre from the car, unless you are travelling extremely slowly. Your reaction time is not going to be quick enough to at least not knock someone over before even realising they are there."

In 2005, NSW's senior deputy state coroner, Jacqueline Milledge, recommended that four-wheel drives weighing two tonnes or more be banned from school grounds and within 200 metres of schools. She also recommended that the drivers be required to hold special licences after five-year-old Bethany Holder was run over by the driver of a Nissan Patrol with a bullbar.

Due to their weight and the bullbars being positioned at perfect head and chest height, drivers of vehicles hit side-on by four-wheel drives are 26 times more likely to be killed or suffer serious injury than if they had been hit by a standard-sized passenger vehicle, according to ABC's *Catalyst* program.

But apparently they're fashionable. If pick-up at your school is a procession of kids being collected from school in a car the size of a three-bedroom house, you may want to consider the values of that school.

Will it take a four-wheel drive to back over the child of another four-wheel drive-owner for these status-obsessed fashion slaves to realise that these vehicles are potential killers?

Here's a cheaper alternative to buying a four-wheel drive. Just buy a normal-sized car and put a sticker on the back that reads: "I DON'T GIVE A STUFF ABOUT YOU AND I VOTE."

Cycling I

I've had a gutful of the "cyclists are a menace" comments that I am hearing from uptight white honkies. A car cuts them off? The driver is a dickhead. A cyclist cuts them off? ALL cyclists are menaces and they should ALL be off the road and NONE OF THEM should be allowed to breed. Here's the truth: cars kill, injure, annoy, abuse, cut off and hassle far more cyclists than vice versa. And if you don't believe me, get on a bike.

There are thugs, lunatics, idiots and morons in all areas of life and cycling is no exception. So why is the odd maverick Lycra-lout not simply viewed as an exception rather than an accurate representation of the entire cycling community?

You think the Hell Ride goes along Beach Road every Sunday? You should talk to some of the mums and dads, commuters and students who pedal during peak hour and they'll tell you stories of road rage that will make you think every day is a hell ride for them.

I want to say thank you. To all the cyclists getting out there in the wind and the cold and the rain and pedalling to work or school or to get about their daily business. They are cutting down on road congestion, helping the environment, freeing up parking spots and reducing their stress levels through both exercise and the financial bonus of a cheaper form of transport.

Many households could (and do) solve the "no time to exercise, can't afford a second car and no parking at work" equation with a bicycle. Others solve it by buying a second car that they can't afford, which contributes to the national debt and in turn inflation and then up goes the interest rates as well as our carbon emissions.

Lay off the cyclists. They should be paid for commuting. We should be standing at the traffic lights handing them drinks and giving them towels when they arrive at work. The government should be doing everything in its power to encourage and facilitate safe cycling in our glorious city.

Good news. Cycling is not just the new golf. Bicycles are the new cars. Australians have been buying more bicycles than cars for the past seven years. More good news. The British Medical Association found that the risk of inactivity is 20 times greater than the health risk posed by a potential accident on a bike.

According to Bicycle Victoria, cycling numbers along Swanston Street (Melbourne's cycling spine) have grown 680 per cent in 15 years. Cycle awareness will increase the more people cycle. People are more conscious of cyclists if their partner, their parent, their sibling, their mate, their children or themselves are out on the road pedalling.

A wonderful culture of cycling is flourishing. A few weeks ago I saw a line of peak-hour traffic create a wider berth than was necessary for the stream of cyclists as the road narrowed. And whoever is behind the free bike-repairs at the north gate of Carlton Gardens every Sunday should be hoisted onto a sedan chair and given some kind of civic reception.

On 28 May 2006, the first Cyclovia in Melbourne was held. Cyclovia means "life to the streets" and it's been happening for more than 30 years around the world. A section of Sydney Road was closed off to cars from 8 am to 2 pm and people cycled, rollerbladed and strolled. All you could hear was the clicking of gears and the whoosh of bike tyres. It was bloody marvellous.

Between 1974 and 2003, travel to school by car rose from 22.6 per cent to 70 per cent. Children being driven to school account for 18 per cent of peak-hour traffic in Melbourne. We are constantly being told that children are getting fatter and driving cars is now the environmental equivalent to piping cigarette smoke into humidicribs. Yet there are still plenty of people who could easily walk or ride their children to school at least a couple of times a week who don't, simply because they can't be bothered. The most effective way parents can encourage children to ride bikes is by riding bikes themselves.

Children should be encouraged to think of their bikes not just as fun and exercise but transport. The Japanese believe that by carrying their babies on their backs it teaches the child when to bow. I suggest that parents riding with their children in baby seats and on tagalongs gives children an instinctive understanding of the flow of traffic. Keep in mind that I have no facts to back that up; it's just what I reckon. I suppose that's why this page is called "Opinion."

Cycling II

Men could never get into Pilates. Why? Not enough stuff to buy. How many yoga mats and pairs of Thai fisherman pants can you have? That's why blokes love cycling. Ride for an hour, come home and then spend five hours trawling the net for the perfect high-modulus-weave carbon-fibre seat post.

Is it my imagination, or is the world being taken over by Lycra louts with their arses in the air, their handlebars on the bitumen and their anti-erectile-dysfunction gel inserts firmly installed?

My partner is mad for it. I realised this, not when I woke one morning to find "boys from the bunch" drinking coffee and comparing pubic-bone heights. And it wasn't when he sat up all night watching the Tour de France in full cycling gear complete with silly little cap, saying the word *peloton* a lot. I realised he was obsessed when he wheeled out his bike and sheepishly asked, in a "Does my bum look big in this?" voice, "Are these carbon-fibre shifters too much with the silver alloy components and the shallow-bend handlebars?"

I smiled, backed away slowly and ran screaming: "FREAK! FREAK! THE MAN IN THE LYCRA WITH THE SHAVED LEGS IS A FREAK!"

At 8 am in his bike gear he's not going anywhere, he's "just done a quick 100 kilometres in a bunch with Cadel Evans." This from a man who used to drive up to the shops to buy his family-size block of Cadbury Dairy Milk.

Suddenly it's all bike bling and cycling porn. Our bedroom is knee-deep in magazines with articles like "Hot Pumps, Top Routes and Tight Quads!" "Chicks Who Like Their Saddles with Titanium Rails" and "Check out the oversized tubing on that, lads!" Some Christians have the letters WWJD (What Would Jesus Do) tattooed on their wrist. My partner has the letters WWLAD (What Would Lance Armstrong Do).

Cycling keeps you fit, saves the planet and gives men the opportunity to wear fluorescent yellow. But, man, is it boring to watch. If you don't believe me, check out *Cycling Central*. "Coming up in today's exciting show: people riding up hills, people riding down hills, and some people riding slightly faster than others." It's the difference between watching a sport and a game. Cycling is a sport. Golf is a game. Put that on your knicks, Bracksy.

There is no larger distance than the distance between people who would rather poke themselves in the eye with a pencil than watch this and cycling freaks. There's no biffo, the bingles are few and far between and when they happen you actually feel them because everyone has been eight years old and come a cropper fanging down a hill. The "exciting attacks" look like one snail going a little less slow than the other. If you know your pubic-bone height, tune into *Cycling Central* and you'll thank me. Also a great watch for the cycling obsessed is *Sooty Park*. It's a magazine-style cycling show that covers everything from couriers to recumbents. Less bling, more fun and a few laughs. Kind of the poor man's bicycle version of *Top Gear*.

Water

Forget sex, politics and religion. Try water. I have tackled plenty of divisive topics in my time and never have I felt so strongly about nailing my colours to the mast to ensure that there is no doubt where my loyalties lie. I am not a Wally with water. I am the stingiest, tightest water miser you will find in the world. Our water bill is on the fridge. Not to remind us to pay it, but so that people can see that our water usage is down 15 per cent from this time last year. And that even though we are a five-person household with a medium-sized garden, we have the typical water consumption (319 litres a day) of a one-person household with a medium-sized garden. I know you're impressed. I'm loving myself stupid.

The other day I overheard someone say: "Soon we'll be flushing the toilet with the bath water." Soon? Did you say soon? We've been flushing the toilet with bath water for a good 18 months. We had a water tank installed seven years ago. We have the most efficient front-loading washing machine available on the market, and we only run it when it's full and even then on the eco cycle. We wash our clothes only if they walk, talk or stink. Odd days or even days? We don't even water our garden. And where's our medal?

I'm pretty laid back with most things. Flossing? Nah. Pelvic-floor exercises? Bugger off. Seatbelt? Only if there's a matching bag. But water wasters? Oooh, they make my blood boil more than a talkback caller from Hoppers Crossing. Bring back capital punishment, flog them, stone them, make them wear a sandwich board saying: "I'm ignorant and greedy." People who say: "Yeah, well I'm not giving my 20-minute shower up for anyone." What judge in this land would punish me for killing people like that? I should be hoisted in a sedan chair as people chant: "She is Lord! She is Lord!"

Comedian Peter Grace has a great line: "People ask how old I am, and I tell them that I'm old enough to remember when a litre of milk was more expensive than a litre of water." Water's going to be more expensive? Good. Overdue correction. It's been too cheap for too long. We have been allowed sinfully to waste our precious drinking water. I'm a fan of rationing. Seriously. A hundred litres a day per person and any more, you pay $2 a litre. I want it to be so expensive that people are smuggling in water and it is only able to be found during a cavity search.

Recycled waste? As long as there are no lumps, bring it on, I say. I won't be happy until five-year-olds are sitting on Father Christmas's knee and when he asks them what they want for Christmas they answer: "A bath. And some rain for the farmers."

Now I could be wrong (but let's face it, that's never happened before), but there have been more than 10,000 written warnings to people about wasting water in Victoria but no fines. Not one. If I were in charge, water wasters would be culled like vermin. "Freeze! Water patrol! Operation Wet and Wild. Drop the hand-held hose not fitted with the required trigger nozzle being used on an unauthorised day." Personally, I think that people caught hosing their footpaths should be hung, drawn and quartered. Remember Operation Noah, dob in a druggie? I vote for Operation Glenda. Dob in a Water Wally.

Water saving has become an extreme sport: "I always use half flush."

"Oh, well, we have composting toilets."

"Well, I haven't showered since the gas crisis in 1998 and I drink my own urine."

People no longer brag about their shagger's back but their bucket back. Tony Martin even did a song called "The Bucket Back Song." And guess what? My mum was in it. I could burst with pride.

My kids' only water luxury is on hot days they get a spray bottle full of water to take in the car to keep cool, because my car doesn't have air-conditioning. It also counts as their bath. And their weekly drinking water allocation.

Didn't Fitzroy get stroppy when it was shamed, along with Caroline Springs, as being one of the suburbs with the biggest water increase? I was so relieved that it wasn't us. But then spewing that we weren't one of the suburbs getting the elephant stamp for being one of the best.

Why was there a public list of the suburbs of shame (which are only a tiny part of the problem), yet the identity of the biggest industrial waster wasters remains a mystery? I call for the naming and shaming of the biggest water wasters in industry and business so that we can boycott their products. Vigilante, or concerned citizen? You choose.

An Atheist for Jesus

After years of discussion by theologians, the Catholic and Anglican churches may be closer to reuniting than ever before. So the big question is, will we be called Anglicaths, Cathligans or Angolics?

Actually, the big question really is: "Is this really important to the people in the pews?" And here's the answer. No. It's not.

A good mate and I, both raised Catholic, were once discussing religion. The outcome of this philosophical debate was that I would quite happily put a dildo and an inflatable sex doll on a church altar, but he couldn't. I said, "Hang on. I pray, I believe in God and I considered myself Catholic, and you're an atheist."

He replied: "I know, but it doesn't stop me from being scared."

My point was that if God is everywhere, no place was more sacred than any other. And yes, I was a teeny bit drunk.

I don't believe in God any more. I'm a cultural Catholic. I couldn't swear on the Bible, I'd have to take an oath on *New Scientist*.

You may laugh, and I wouldn't blame you, but my faith was ultimately challenged, not by the unequal distribution of wealth and suffering in the world. And not by genital mutilation inflicted on children in the name of God.

I started questioning the existence of God as I explained Bible stories to my children. "So Mary was a virgin and an angel appeared before her and told her that she was going to have a baby and he was the son of God. When he grew up he walked on water, fed a massive crowd with a few loaves of bread and couple of fish, turned water into wine and then they nailed him on to a wooden cross and he died. Then he came back to life. Actually, hang on guys, this sounds like a crock."

And before you start writing letters, I don't need saving. I'm not having a go at anyone else's faith here; this is simply a comment on my own. And I am sure that if you have faith, any rigorous discussion will not anger or offend you, it will just strengthen your own faith. Faith is a personal and private thing. I'm going to make like the late comedian Bill Hicks and say, "If you don't like what I say about God, then forgive me."

Being a parent made me see what a comfort it is for children to believe that now that nanna has passed on she is in a wonderful place where she can play bingo with her mates all day, eat cake and never get fat. As opposed to "Nanna died screaming in pain, she'll be eaten by worms or burnt to a crisp and we'll never see her again."

Before science really got cracking, people thought the world was flat, that disabled children were born as punishment and that babies died because of teething. I understand how the poor unwashed masses could believe this stuff. And how and why the powers that be could use the existence of God, heaven and hell effectively to keep them in line.

I was never given an option with religion, I was just handed a scapular and told I was a Catholic. Many people are left with a crumbling ruin of the faith they were raised with. Some parts have fallen off, toppled over and others been strategically dismantled while others are conveniently preserved. I'm not married; don't believe in God; yet my children are baptised. And I'm not alone.

How can I take my three boys to church when they'll ask why priests are all male and I'll have to tell them that chicks are not up to scratch? The token nod of altar girls is not enough. When, as a 12-year-old, I got a whiff of this radical new opportunity, I asked our parish priest if I could be an altar girl and he said: "We don't do that kind of thing here." When I asked why, he just said, "We just don't." I'm not bitter. It gave me hard evidence of the misogyny in the church that I had always sensed. Isn't the refusal to allow female priests against equal opportunity laws or is there a disclaimer on faith-based phallocracy?

If the top dogs in the Catholic church are going to be presumptuous enough to "interpret" the Bible to prevent women from becoming priests because of whatever religion-approved sexism they have conveniently manipulated, I wonder if they would be so kind as to interpret the following:

> No man who has any defect may come near [the altar of God]: no man who is blind or lame, who is hunchbacked or dwarfed, or who has any eye defect, or who has festering or running sores or damaged testicles.
>
> Leviticus 21:19–21

Take note, short-sighted priests.

I believe that Jesus Christ lived. And he said great things. So maybe I can follow the example of Christ and be an atheist. I may not believe in God any more, but I do believe strongly and deeply in love and truth, despite the absence of any scientific proof.

Chocolate Jesus

I don't know much about 91-kilogram chocolate statues of Jesus, but I know what I like. When I heard about the giant edible Christ, I badly wanted to make like an Easter egg and smash it on my forehead. Or better still, bite off both ends and suck my coffee through it.

The exhibit of a 1.8-metre chocolate statue of Jesus has angered Catholics, but had this cultural Catholic laughing so hard I almost spat out the coffee scroll in the shape of the Virgin Mary that I was eating. And when I read that the artwork was titled "My Sweet Lord", I almost needed to be resuscitated.

Members of the US Catholic League were outraged by this artwork by Cosimo Cavallaro and I can only assume that it was because it was made from milk chocolate and not 70 per cent couverture dark chocolate. Then I thought they were angry because they couldn't find "91-kilogram chocolate statue of Jesus" on the Weight Watchers list. American Cardinal Edward Egan described it as sickening and I can't help agreeing with him. I can't even get through half an Elegant Rabbit without wanting to have my stomach pumped.

Lines just kept popping into my head: "Just like a chocolate milkshake, only Jesus," and "Helps you work, rest and pray." All jokes aside, I wonder if chocolate Jesus tastes exactly like chicken.

Not only did these fanatics boycott the New York hotel exhibiting "My Sweet Lord", but there were death threats. Death threats? I missed that commandment: Thou Shalt Not Kill Unless Chocolate Statues of Religious Figures Are Involved. If this exhibition was happening in Australia there'd be no death threats; we'd be rocking up and having our photos taken with a chip off the old family block. Because Aussie Catholics can take a joke. (Note to self: MUST CALL GEORGE PELL)

Sorry, here comes another one: "I Can't Believe It's Not Jesus!"

Don't you think that they are over-reacting just a tad? Are we sitting at the kids' table or up with the adults? The artist made the statue as a tribute. Why are these fanatics up in arms over a block of chocolate? I think that it's all claptrap and mumbo-jumbo myself, but what has the artist's relationship with Jesus got to do with them? Do they own Christ? If Cavallaro goes to hell for upsetting God, that's his problem.

Prayer is simply the notion of transcending the physical, so how can 91 kilos of chocolate offend the sensibilities of Christians?

Why are they afraid? What's the fear? If we laugh, then what next? People will stop turning up to church? Well, it's too late for that. Why are they so defensive, so protective? It is a case of "don't you upset the guy in the sky or we'll be the ones who get in trouble." How robust is their faith if it takes a chocolate Jesus to rattle them? Why should any religion be a cordoned-off, joke-free zone? Are they scared that if we push hard enough that it may break and collapse?

Some people are just gagging to be outraged. Check out the statue. If no one had told you, you wouldn't know it was Jesus; it looks like Oprah's old boyfriend, Stedman. Keep in mind that the artist's previous work includes coating an entire house and all its surfaces with spray cheese and covering a four-poster bed with processed ham. I'm not hanging that on my wall.

The US Catholic League's Keira McCaffery said: "Would this art gallery display a naked chocolate statue of Muhammad with his genitals exposed during Ramadan? I think not." And she's right. They probably would be too scared by what happened to Salman Rushdie. But there is an unwritten and moral logic that allows Jews to make fun of Jews, Christians to make fun of Christians and Muslims to make fun of Muslims. It's OK to piss out of the tent but it's not OK to piss in.

It reminds me of the controversy over American photographer Andres Serrano's "Piss Christ", a photograph of a plastic Jesus on a crucifix in a glass of the artist's urine. At the time, art critic and Catholic nun Sister Wendy Beckett said that she approved of the work, considering it a legitimate statement on "what we have done to Christ."

It seems to be fine for some religious folk to sneer and deride other people's faith but you are not allowed to do it to them. Blasphemy seems to be only when someone offends your faith. In the same way all the people who don't endorse capital punishment are quite happy to see Saddam hanging from a noose. Because that's different.

The idea of a chocolate Jesus makes far more sense to me than the alleged resurrection of Christ being celebrated by eggs and rabbits because they symbolise fertility. I thought that the symbol for fertility was Catholic mothers.

Body of Christ? I'll have Top Deck, thanks. Is it a good laugh or is it bad art? Maybe it's both. Happy Easter.

Salacious Headlines

I recently found myself in the gift shop of the Museum of Modern Art in New York. As I wandered along the vast wealth of superb books, I couldn't help noticing that the most well-thumbed, almost dog-eared among the thousands of stunning works was a book called *Eroticism & Art*.

That's right. Porn. Well not exactly porn, but porn thinly veiled as culture. Art? Literature? Design? Architecture? Maybe, just ask us after we've flicked through the dicks and the titties. Not buying it, of course. Just having a quick squiz when no one is watching.

Here's a quiz. Which of the following has *not* been one of the most viewed articles in the online edition of a Fairfax publication in the past month or so?

Man Crushed by Flying Cow.
Uncle Bites Nephew.
Mum Jailed for Making Kids Act Retarded.
Rear-end "Facials": the Cheek of it All.

Father Charged after Baby Burnt in Microwave.
Kevin Rudd's Popularity Soars.
Throat Cancer Caused by Oral Sex.
Teenager Decapitates Mother and Takes Severed Head to Internet Lounge.
Hair Regrown in Baldness Breakthrough.
Man Attempts Suicide by Chewing through His Own Arteries.
Sordid Salad Tosser Avoids Jail.

The one not in the most viewed list? That's right, the one about Kevin Rudd's popularity. The rest have all made the list. I find it fascinating, almost addictive, checking out the most viewed articles of online newspapers. It's like having a stickybeak through the collective readership's rubbish. The front page suggests that what we all want to read in the big newspaper with the big words is "Howard's Decline," "Global Warming" and "War in Iraq." But according to the most viewed articles, you'll find that we're more interested in reading about the new hot-dog scoffing world champion, the man sprung caught having sex with a guinea pig or the patient whose genitals caught fire after he passed wind during laser treatment.

Are the hundreds of worthy but unread books on display in people's homes the equivalent of the large bowl of uneaten fruit trying to distract from the chocolate wrappers stuffed under the seat of our cars? Which are the stick mags stashed in the back of our filing cabinet, the celeb mags in our toilet or that Ikea catalogue on our bedside table?

Some news we want to read, some we should be reading and some we need to read. With the evolution of online content we can now see what people are actually reading.

Or can we? What we do know is that we are not alone about wanting to read about the mother who ate her baby. People will argue that the "most viewed" and "most emailed" lists only reveal that online readers are reading the sensational stories, but that's bollocks. Humans are drawn to the titillating, the salacious and the extremes of human behaviour.

The bottom line is that these horrifying, debauched and fascinating stories are fine to read. All as part of a balanced reading diet. They are the dim sims of the newspaper world. Enticing? Sure. But of no real nutritional value. And let's face it, if we were just after these kinds of stories we'd be reading *Take 5*, *That's Life* or *National Enquirer*, not the *Age*.

The danger is whether supposedly being able to see what people are reading is dictating the content we are being dished up. Now the powers that be can clearly see what people are into, is it affecting the quality of newspapers and the nature of news? In a word? Yes. Newspapers are businesses: they find a market and cater to demand. So are readers finally getting what they deserve, or is this unreliable reflection of our news consumption leading the print media to think this is all readers want? And should therefore be given – but in a broadsheet format purely for the cred.

Take a moment to think about the handful of words that would make the most eye-catching headline. The headline that you would hate yourself for being compelled to read: Pope's Giant Porn Stash. Warney–Vanstone Sex Tape. Princess Mary Drug Scandal. Dead Baby Found in Bin.

Sure, you'd read the story. You'd eat your dessert first. But you would then eat your veggies. Wouldn't you?

Media are continuing to change dramatically as the gathering and dissemination of news is being radically transformed. Pretty soon the six o'clock news will be a thing of the past as people cherry-pick their news when and where they feel like it. Newspapers have been forced to become extremely canny about how to keep their readership up and the art of the punchy headline has become more important than ever.

Congratulations to the clever online folk coming up with even funnier headlines. You are certainly amusing me. $100 says this article will end up in the most emailed list because it ends up with a titillating headline.

Do Not Call Register

I was delighted by Bill Heffernan's comments last week about Julia Gillard. It was refreshing to hear a politician refusing to veil his deep-seated misogyny and archaic views with words like "family values," "Christian ethics" and "decency." More please. Say it like you see it, you old dinosaur.

Personally I don't think that Gillard is unfit to lead the country because she has decided not to have children. I think that she is unfit to lead the country because she has red hair. Gillard is as smart as a whip and brimming with intellect, vision, imagination, dedication and passion, but let's face it, she is a chick. And we can't be having that in politics, because who knows where we'd end up?

Best we continue to reassure ourselves with ye olde worlde rhetoric that we are "world class" and are the only nation to believe in "a fair go" and "mateship." We should keep letting the middle-aged white blokes in grey suits run the joint because they are doing a ripper job decimating eduction, healthcare and the environment. I doubt any woman could do a better job. Apart, perhaps, from Helen Coonan, the genius behind the Do Not Call Register.

My name is not in the phone book, but my partner's name is. When I answer the phone and someone says "Hello, Mrs Borg?" I respond: "I'm sorry, she's dead." Because that's the name of my partner's mother, who is dead. And I hang up. As I am putting the receiver down, I hear most of the cold callers say, "That's OK, I'm just calling to offer you some unique dining opportunities in your area."

When I heard about the Do Not Call Register I was thrilled. After registering, I read the fine print and wondered why I bothered.

Here is a list of the bodies who are still allowed to interrupt your sleep, your dinner, your quality time with loved ones, your bath, your space and your peace: charities or charitable institutions, educational institutions, religious organisations, government bodies, registered political parties, independent members of parliament, political candidates and market and social researchers. Why are they exempt? Anyone?

Don't feed me some garbage about them being in the public interest. They're not. They're in their own interest. With email, SMS, snail mail, people shaking cans, holding clipboards, information packs and balloons for kiddies in the street, as well as people turning up to our front doors, why should anyone be allowed to invade our space by calling us? Simple answer? They shouldn't.

When the phone rings, it could be important. The groups exempted from the Do Not Call Register should not be able to prioritise their message to interrupt whatever we are doing to ask us to sell a book of raffle tickets for cats with no heads. Or to tell us why we should vote for them. People should only be allowed to call us if and when it suits us. Send us an email or a letter and we'll get to it when we can be bothered. It's easier to delete an email or bin some marketing or campaigning than it is to tell someone on the phone to bugger off. Unless, of course, you're me.

Our lives are so full of things blinking at us to tell us to charge them, download them, read them and respond to them that it's an infringement on our privacy to have anyone calling us unless we have specifically given them our phone number.

How keen are the public not to receive calls from people that they don't know about things they don't give a stuff about? So keen that the $33-million Do Not Call Register crashed just after it was launched last week, due to the enormous demand.

So why has all this money gone into something that will achieve only slightly less than bugger all? The public has said, loud and clear, "we don't want cold calls," and the government has responded by saying: "Yes, we hear you. But we'll totally disregard what you want and force on you what it suits us for you to have."

Can anyone explain to me why registering on the Do Not Call Register lasts only three years? Because you can deregister any time, just in case you start missing some guy from Delhi calling to find out if you are not satisfied, somewhat satisfied, satisfied, very satisfied or extremely satisfied with your current mobile phone plan. Just as you've sat down to dinner.

Instead of setting up a Do Not Call Register, they should have set up a Do Call Register. Then no one could receive any cold calls unless they'd registered for them. People would be able to choose who could call them and when. I'd tick the box that said Calls from Bill Heffernan, because I could do with a good laugh any time of day or night.

IQ Tests

I read this article in a rival newspaper. I am not proud of it, it is just that I was at the doctor and it was the only thing to read apart from half-a-dozen copies of *That's Life* and the Christmas edition of *Knitters' Monthly*. Anyways, I read this article about how IQ tests are supposedly culturally specific, elitist and an inaccurate reflection of someone's intelligence. I vividly remember thinking, "Mmmm. I hope I remembered to pull those snags out of the freezer."

But the article got me thinking about how intelligent I am. I can't get through my week without *Foreign Correspondent* but I adore *Australia's Funniest Home Videos*. I know that Bambang Yudhoyono is the President of Indonesia yet I constantly put my shoes on the wrong feet. I am crap at Trivial Pursuit although I would feel quite confident having a convo with Glenn Ridge.

Am I a genius or do I have the intellectual capacity of 350 grams of poor quality chuck steak?

My parents have both done IQ tests but I don't know their scores. They strongly believed that it was unethical to reveal information that might mislead children into forming inaccurate assumptions about gender-specific capabilities. I respect them for that. Mum said "Both your father and I know our IQs. We will not tell you what they are. But mine is higher." My parents were keen for us to have our own opinions – as long as we remained Labor-voting, church-going, Catholic heterosexual carnivores who barracked for Collingwood.

I knew nothing about IQ tests, so I quizzed people. Curiously, the only people who had done an IQ test and could recollect anything about it were people who had scored high IQs. These people blurted out "Mine is 188 and I have had it tested twice so I know it is accurate" as soon as I mentioned the letter "I" let alone "Q." One wanker assured me that he had an IQ that would get him into Mensa. "Yeah right," I said, "only if they needed some plastering done and you were the cheapest quote."

Even then, when I asked these intellectual giants with photographic memories what you actually did in an IQ test they were extremely vague – almost conspiratorial. "I can't really remember, I don't know, the kind of tests where you, sort of, complete the sequence."

"What? Like: lady is hot, lady walks over to fridge, lady cracks open a cold beer, clock shows two hours pass and lady is now swinging from chandelier?"

"Mmmm, no. Not exactly."

"Well then what?"

"IQ test?" says my friend Tim, "You just did one. If you voted yes in the republic referendum you passed."

It became clear that only by going through the magic tunnel and joining the secret club would I ever find out what you actually did in an IQ test. I had no option but to take the plunge.

But where do you get it? The House of IQ? IQs Are Us? Jim's mobile IQ testing? So I called my old psychologist Ivan: if anyone would know he would. (Oh yes, I've had therapy, how else do you think I managed to stop stalking Eddie McGuire.) "Yep, you've come to the right place, psychologists administer these tests. Call this mate of mine Frank, he'll do it for you. I'd love to but I think I might be biased."

Well, it seemed that at least one of us was confident I was a genius.

So I called Frank and booked in. It would take about three hours over two sessions – could I do it tomorrow? Sure. Would I need to bring anything? Do I need anything to assist me to read? "Yes," I said. "Bold type, plenty of pictures and a facilitator."

On the other side of the line I heard a groan.

I got very excited and I realised that I didn't care what the result was as long as I wasn't normal. I wanted either to be right up there with Stephen Hawking or "CATHERINE IS IT? LET US KNOW IF WE ARE TALKING TOO FAST FOR YOU."

It was at this point that I had to ask myself, do I believe in IQ tests? Like Valentine's Day, the monarchy and horoscopes, if there was something in it for me, shit yeah, I'd believe in them. It didn't take long for me to decide that I was, more than likely, a genius, so I got onto the internet to find out how to join Mensa.

I spent a bit of time browsing around the site, it was interesting to note that according to the Australian Mensa site, "You're sure to find like-minded people at a Mensa event. Perhaps you just want to relax and exchange repartee with others who'll get your jokes and add their own quips. Many find Mensa a welcome relief." Hold me back, let's party.

Did you know that when you are in Mensa you can stay with Mensarians all over the world? You can. Which is great news if you want to wake up in a musty English cottage and do a cryptic crossword with some professor of medieval poetry who has a brain like Barry Jones. But bad news if it bothers you that she looks like him as well.

When I saw the words Mensa Workout, I thought, "It's not cheating, I'll just see how I go with these questions, purely for research."

The workout took 30 minutes. It promised to give me an accurate indication of whether or not I would make it into Mensa. There were questions like, "If it takes two typists two minutes to type two pages, how long would it talk eight typists to type 14 pages?" and "Which of the following is the odd one out: carrot, potato, turnip, parsnip or onion?" Onion. Definitely. Why? Because I have never heard of an urban myth where someone turned up to casualty saying, "I was standing on the table changing the light globe, nude, fell down and that is how I ended up with an onion rammed up my ..."

I waited patiently while my score was processed and used the time productively by fantasising about quipping along about the latest advances in quantum physics with my new Mensa buddies Edgar, Constance and Mr Lim. The score came through. My biggest nightmare. Stone cold boring normal. On the 52nd percentile.

I was scared. I was panicked. But all was not lost. Didn't I inflate my HSC score reasoning that it was an assessment system that positively discriminated towards Angle Saxon males from high socio-economic demographics? Don't I respond "Doctor" when asked what my title is on the grounds that if people are shallow and superficial enough to grade and treat people according to their education level and perceived class, then I want the best treatment available and will say whatever it takes to get it? Absolutely. So if the score was bad I'd lie. The test was tomorrow.

The morning of the test I remembered that fish was good brain food and although I was tempted to tuck into a bowl of ocean trout and prawn Whiskettes I had Coco Pops for breakfast instead. I drove to Frank's suites and as I was trying to reverse park between a brand new Mercedes and a rust-bucket Datsun Skyline with a canary I found that I was so fired-up and paranoid that I was convinced that I was under surveillance and that this was part of the test.

I entered the building and was ushered into Frank's waiting room where I found myself sitting alone. Frank walked towards me. "Wendy?"

"No, it's Catherine," I said.

"Are you sure?" He quizzed. Was this part of the test?

"Yeah. Pretty sure."

"Do you want tea or coffee?" I was *sure* that this was part of the test.

"Coffee, I mean tea, definitely coffee, is it instant? If that is the case I will have tea. Did I pass?"

I did the first part of the test then and there and the following day I did the second part of the test with his colleague Jan. I have to admit that I really enjoyed it. I loved getting things right and when I got something wrong I took comfort in the fact that I didn't want to be a badly dressed friendless loser genius whose best friend is a first edition of *Faust*.

The test I did was the Wechsler Adult Intelligence Scale Edition III, the latest state-of-the-art IQ test, the Rolls-Royce of IQ tests if you will. Frank assured me that it was very accurate and impossible to manipulate. If someone was trying to fail or cheat there were all these things that would trip them up so that the score would still be accurate. The whole thing was broken down into 11 sub-tests. I'll give you a few examples to give you the general idea.

SUB-TEST A
"OK, Catherine, I will show you a picture and you tell me the main thing that is missing." [Shows a picture of man watching football on television]. "I know! He doesn't have a beer." "No, I am sorry, that's a tricky one, if you look closer you'll see that the television isn't plugged in."

SUB-TEST B
The numbers one to ten were given corresponding symbols and I was then given rows of random numbers and had to write the corresponding symbols below them. If I had a gin and tonic and a packet of Horizon Menthol Lite in front of me I would have sworn that I was "down the bingo."

SUB-TEST C
I was given coloured blocks and shown patterns. I was then asked to arrange the blocks to correspond with the patterns. I kept having to stop myself arranging the blocks to say BOOBS.

SUB-TEST D
"You have given a man a $10 bill to buy a $7 goat. What do you get back?"

"An inexpensive birthday gift for Michael Jackson and enough change to buy half-a-dozen potato cakes."

SUB-TEST E
What is the population of Australia?

"Yobbos."

I also had to repeat sequences of numbers and then repeat sequences of numbers in reverse. I had to tell them what the similarity was between a bird and a shrub, a leg and an arm, and cowardice and courage. I also had to tell them what I would do if I found a friendly dog with a name-tag and phone number on it. Frank was very encouraging. Every now and then when I would get one wrong he would say, "You didn't get that one right – but don't worry you are doing very well." At one stage Frank said to me "Your verbal skills and vocabulary are very good."

"Really? Very good?" I was lapping it up. I knew I was gifted.

"Oh yes, very good – the level of someone who has been to university."

I have been to university.

So it was over. I thanked Frank and Jan. Frank said, "So we will fax the report off to you tomorrow."

"Great, thanks."

"You are writing an article about it, aren't you?"

"Yeah, that's right."

"You're not going to tell people what the questions are, are you?"

"Sorry? What is this, the Masonic handshake or something? It's not illegal, is it?"

"No, it is not illegal, it's just that, you know, we wouldn't want to give anyone an unfair advantage, would we? Maybe you could change the concepts slightly."

"But I thought that this test was foolproof?"

I gave them my word that I wouldn't use the proper test questions but bad luck – I lied.

I went home and waited for my result and for the officials from the Australian Institute of Geniuses to knock on my door and ask me if I would head their space program. Like any superficial competitive person I spent that night tossing and turning, going over the wrong answers that I had given. I kicked myself particularly for responding to the question "Who was the prime minister of England during the Second World War" with the answer "King George III."

I received the 12 pages of results at 8.30 pm the following evening. Obviously Frank doesn't spend his Saturday nights having a few quiet ales and quipping down the local Mensa. "Catherine obtained an IQ of 117 which places her within the *High Average* range of intellectual functioning and above those of 87 per cent of her peers. However, in Catherine's case the IQ is less meaningful because there are large discrepancies ..."

Ripped off. I was *High Average*. This test was rigged. Above the *Average* classification and below the *Superior* one. Now that's what I want to be, *Superior*. How close had I been to *Superior?* Maybe I was *Borderline Superior*. (Surprisingly it never dawned on me that I may have been *Borderline Average*.) So I came to the conclusion that IQ tests were obviously complete crap and I wanted to do one again so I could show that I truly was superior.

I must admit that I was a little deflated by my test result. A couple of days later I was back on the internet and chanced across a stack of free internet IQ tests. Here it was, the second opinion that I was after. Did I have 13 minutes to do an accurate and free test? Sure, and this was going to be my final test. Definitely. This was the one that I was going to believe. So I downloaded it, I stormed through it and came up with an IQ score of 148. Was that good? Put it this way: according to the chart, 130 is genius and 150 is reached by less than half of 1 per cent of all test takers. Now this was my kind of test.

So as you can see, I got better with practice. The 30-minute Mensa Workout said that I had the capacity to follow the plotline of *Neighbours* – but only just. The three-hour test said that I was smart enough to read the newspaper that I write for. But the 13-minute test said that I was quipping standard. My tip? Shop around and find the one you like.

Technology

My five-year-old mate Elliot did a puppet show for his mum and dad yesterday. At the end of it he announced "for more information go to our website wwwdotwwwdotcomwdot-dotwwdot." His mum observed that it was impossible for her and her son to experience the same childhood. Elliot's a very funny kid. At the age of two he hassled his mum to speak to me and when he got on the phone all he said was, "The number you have called is not connected, please check the number and try again."

There is a sign in the library at our kids' school that says something like "technology is a new world. Our children are the native speakers and we adults are the migrants." I was reminded of this when my nine-year-old asked me what a uterus looked like. When I told him that I would draw him a picture he said, "Why don't we just Google images?"

I hate the fact that I do love technology. Because I rely on it so heavily these days. The internet is like having a really smart person in the house all the time: "To cook meatballs in the oven what temperature do I use?" "What does pulchritude mean?" "I need the postcode for Wandiligong" "Was it Zsa Zsa Gabor who said 'You can't send me to jail because I don't like lesbians and I don't eat lasagne'?" Just ask the omniscient World Wide Web.

Email takes many of the daunting shibboleths (I didn't know what that word meant either until I looked it up on dictionary.com) out of modern communications. And I love SMS because it's like passing notes in class. I have been SMSed updates during a friend's first date in London while I was sitting on the couch in Melbourne. I've even been SMSed by people at the same dinner party who were taking the mickey out of the host's stingy servings and right-wing views. You know who you are.

But BTW (By The Way), I won't know if you are going to be l8 (late) or if you will BTWBO (Be There With Bells On) and for all I know you may be ROFL (Rolling On Floor Laughing) because I don't understand any of those AA (Annoying Acronyms). AYSOS (Are You Stupid Or Something) you may ask. Well, it's NMP (Not My Problem) and you should just OMIK (Open Mouth, Insert Keyboard). If you can't be stuffed writing the whole word, don't bother. The only things that annoy me more are those little smiley faces that I have to turn my head 90 degrees to read. Don't be such a control freak about how I interpret what you say. If you are so paranoid about being misunderstood, how about we catch up face to face? Or do you live online these days? What is the postcode for East Cyber Heights?

It makes me sad that my sons' first view of pornography will be on a computer screen, and not from a 1979 Penthouse Gold Label Edition handed down from generation to generation and viewed in a tent at a sleepover. We no longer hear the thud of the wad of photos land on the kitchen table with 24 or 36 random images of events or moments long gone. I was so late moving over to digital that I'd snap a shot with our negative camera and visiting kids would turn the camera around and be stunned that they couldn't view the photo I'd had just taken.

Technology has its swings and roundabouts. One of the most underestimated benefits of the cyber-world is its ability to embrace people, and to help them find more same and less different. People suffering rare diseases or folks with obscure interests can create a little club regardless of geographical restrictions or social awkwardness.

Sure, "oversharing" online is tragic, but there's no gun to your head to go to grouphug.com. One of my favourite examples of the internet's capacity for catharsis is PostSecret (postsecret.blogspot.com). Anonymous secrets are sent in on a postcard, exhibited online and changed weekly. It is like having an X-ray into people's souls. You realise how much we have in common and how fragile we all are. Like you, I have hundreds of secrets, I just can't pick which one to send.

The Thank You Project (thankyouproject.com.au) collects messages of thanks. On 1 June, these messages will be simultaneously projected into the night sky in Sydney, Melbourne and Brisbane. Join this online community and say a simple and heartfelt "thank you." To someone. Or for something. I sent three. You can't underestimate the power of this simple act of gratitude, all thanks to the fancy, whiz-bang computer.

Australian comedy

*

The Wedge

You know what I would love to be writing today? "See the new sketch show *The Wedge*? Brilliant! I'm so thrilled that there is something for young comedy writers to aspire to and a show to hang out to watch."

Stand by and watch me commit career suicide. I am prepared to be a martyr for the cause. Just call me Blessed Dev of Coburg.

I did a few weeks' writing for *The Wedge* but you will be pushed to find a word of my stuff on screen. This is because when they said, "What we are after is new, fresh and young," I didn't realise that what they actually meant was "boring, safe and dumbed down." Most of the scripts have been rewritten so many times that the guts of the joke has been diluted severely or obliterated entirely.

There are moments of brilliance in *The Wedge* and they shine like jewels, tantalising us with the promise of what it could be. The performers are gifted, the writers solid and the directors talented. The problem is that the producers and network execs are trying to please too many people and offend the least at the same time. It's that old lowest common denominator equals broader audience equation.

If I had another 500 words I would love to explain how these decisions are made but really it is just as complex, illogical and frustrating as the process at your work. The people in charge can be creative bullies, creative magicians or creative midwives. And just like your work, in Tellyland we have egotistical, phallocratic, narrow-minded control freaks with delusions of intellectualism and extremely bad hair.

If I were the only person disillusioned by *The Wedge* I would reserve my judgement. But I am not. I have been astonished by the number of people who have been frothing at the mouth to voice their disappointment and disgust at such shoddy work. You've squandered a brilliant opportunity to create jobs and showcase our artists. This show will not be the highlight of anyone's career.

I want our industry to thrive, not just so we all have work but so that as a viewer I have something to watch. I would rather my children watch a stunning import than half-baked home-grown stuff. Even if I have to remind them that it's "rubbish," "bum" and "lollies" not "trash," "butt" and "candy."

Shows such as *The Wedge* don't do our comedy industry any favours. It discourages networks from investing in Australian comedy and viewers from supporting it. I have been writing for television for 14 years and I can confidently say that our industry is better than this.

The Wedge is not going to be a memorable show, which is not to say it is not going to be a long-running show. And that is not to say that it isn't going to get better. It needs inspired creative control, guts and instinct.

It's sad to think that shows such as *League of Gentlemen*, *The Office* and *Big Train* would never get up in Australia. But it's promising that *Frontline*, *Kath & Kim*, *We Can Be Heroes* and *The Chaser's War on Everything* have.

Thank God You're Here

The bad news is I'm not here to talk about myself. Hey, it's OK. Deep breath. Let it go. The good news is that I am here to talk about those born-to-rule private-school princes from Working Dog and their latest sacrifice to the unwashed masses. The suburban herds they probably wouldn't cross the road to spit on if they were on fire. But let's be honest here, who would?

If you haven't checked out *Thank God You're Here* on Channel Ten, Wednesday nights at 7.30, tune in, chill out and watch the most un-Australian concept on Australian television: an Australian concept. It's quality family entertainment, which is a welcome change from the usual family entertainment at our place, which generally consists of stapling my children's lips together.

Basically, the show's format is: a performer enters a room and has to bluff through a situation they know nothing about. On paper it sounds like a day in the life of Alexander Downer, but you'll be relieved to know it's not as excruciating as that. It's a format that showcases the skill of performers in the gentle art of bullshitting. The words "reality television" have been thrown around to describe *TGYH* but it doesn't really fit. I have created another genre. Ready? Improtainment. It's the words improvisation and entertainment fused. You don't need to tell me – I know, I'm a genius.

You can't go that wrong when you have Shane Bourne as your host. Shane is a talented performer and a generous host, plus he has the number-one quality that Australians admire: he is not up himself. This man is above and beyond television and comedy aristocracy. He represents everything this industry should be about: irreverence, intelligence and well-placed dick jokes. We loved him in *MDA* as much as we loved him on *Hey Hey*, sitting next to Maurie Fields doing: "Two women. One man. Big problem. Lights go out. Bigger problem." He has won AFIs, has been around since the Datsun Stanza and still manages to look like he loves what he does and enjoys the audience.

The first show's line-up was Frank Woods, Peter Rowsthorn, Angus Sampson and Fifi Box. Now, I'm not proud of it, but I must admit that when I saw Fifi in the ensemble I, like every other overweight suburban mother with stretch marks and issues with anger thought: "Where's Andrea Powell, Rebecca De Unamuno, Julia Zemiro or Roz Hammond? Why another cute blonde with a bubbly disposition?" and couldn't wait to rip into her. But I must admit, I was very surprised. Frank went for the big laughs, Pete was solid, but Fifi was very strong and came across as the person who most played the game.

Last week's show was just as entertaining: Angus really hit the mark and Shaun Micallef did what he does best – bumble around like a hapless academic shooting out perfectly crafted lines. Bert's son Mathew Newton was a lovely addition and Fifi proved the first show wasn't a fluke.

She has what it takes to succeed in television: the ability to talk under wet cement. I know what you're thinking: "sounds lowest common denominator," "it's not what you'd call cutting-edge television," "is her name really Fifi Box?" Sure, it's not *The Office*, it's not *Six Feet Under*, but it's not *Friday Night Games*, either. What is most appealing about this show is that it's not trying to be anything it isn't. The fascination of reality television is watching people thinking on their feet and reacting to situations they are not prepared for. *TGYH* has these elements without the ritual humiliation on-screen and the self-loathing most viewers suffer after watching an episode of *The Biggest Loser.*

What makes this show work is the team's creative control, which is something desperately lacking in this industry. Too many shows are moulded by what producers think the network execs think the viewers want. It reminds me of the old joke. Question: What's a camel? Answer: A horse designed by committee. *Thank God You're Here* is a horse.

Working Dog make great products. You can tell these are people who really like making television, and not just pumping out SOS – the Same Old Shit. My only gripe would be Tom Gleisner's judging. When you have everyone flying by the seat of their pants, it's quite clunky to have such tightly scripted judging. Having a couple of judges with a comic bent might work a little better, but what would I know?

Nick Giannopoulos

Dear Nick Giannopoulos,

Again with the wog! You've got your *Wogs Out of Work*, you've got your *Wog-A-Rama*, you've got your *Wog Boy* and now you've got your *Wog Story*!

You are a *Hey Hey It's Better Wogs and Gardens* away from being labelled a one-trick pony. Not that I have any problems with one-trick ponies. Lily Brett? Brilliant writer, a dialogue genius, one-trick pony. Jerry Seinfeld? Superlative comedian, perfect timing, one-trick pony. Phar Lap? Nice horse, fast runner, one-trick pony.

So if that's the case, what is the problem that almost everyone – OK, I'll stop watering it down just in case I meet you – absolutely everyone has with you?

Is it simply a matter of time until we are furnished with such cultural monuments as *The Year My Wog Broke*, *My Left Wog* and *The Unbearable Lightness of Wog*? Will we be fortunate enough to experience *Full Metal Wog*, *Gone with the Wog* and *The Nutty Wog*?

And if it's true that you have patented the wog word, this piece will probably not be published due to unlicensed use of the word wog. But if it is published, I'd like to make it clear that considering the patenting I am very much looking forward to purchasing The New Holden Wog with free air, Whirlpool's new 7-kilo, frontloading Wog and the new Victa two-stroke Wog.

And before you jump to any assumptions, let me confirm that I am one of those inner-city, caffe-latte-drinking types who you reckon hate your stuff. But you are wrong – I like your stuff; very funny. I just have a couple of hot tips for you Nicky, from all of us, because you obviously don't have any really good friends brave enough to tell you to pull your head in:

1. Don't pretend to be an artist when you are just into marketing. You're a marketing man and there is nothing wrong with that. Stand and be proud. You're not poisoning babies, you're just trying to make a couple of mill. You are funny and quite a competent writer and actor, but you are not an artist. An artist does not stand at the Logies and bang on about the popularity of his work (by the way, Nick, the Logies speech? We're waiting for the punchline).

2. You will never own the word wog. You want to get off racism and have an integrated society? Wouldn't it make more sense to dilute the power of the word by overuse? Tell everyone to use it, all the time. Declaring yourself the sole authorisation point for use of the word (like you did with Liz Hayes on *60 Minutes*) is like saying "guns are destructive but I want to be the only one to have one." The attitude of discrimination that made you want revenge is the same one you are fostering with such exclusionism.

The word wog can be used with deep intention and with vicious malice. It's just a word. The intent is the problem. How would I know? Well, my son is half wog and my partner is 100 per cent proof (as I have said before, he was a wog even before you, mate). The kids I went to school with (Macedonian, Yugoslav, Croatian, Italian, Greek, Lebanese, etc) were fiercely proud of being wogs and felt it was a genuine term of respect. "We're wogs mate, we got culture. What are you? Stupid skips ..."

Kids in my street in Coburg these days don't even know what the word wog means. In your attempts to subvert the dominant paradigm, you are keeping a calcifying culture on a life-support system to be housed in the comedy anachronism museum with Sir Les Patterson, Ugly Dave Gray and his My-Mother-In-Law-Is-So-Ugly jokes, alongside the dumb Paddy, clueless woman, money-grabbing Jew, smelly Pom, dumb blonde and geeky Asian who can't drive. Don't we want to move on?

3. Stop propagating this myth that the wogs built this country singlehandedly. What about the Irish, the Scots, the English, the Chinese, the indigenous, the Maltese, the Slavs, the Balkans? The list would fill this page. What were they doing? Macrame? The southern European influence on our lives is indisputable and I have an espresso machine on my stove, halumi cheese on my shopping list and the smell of pastitzis on my breath to prove it. But I also have a wok in my cupboard, Guinness in my fridge and a Dutch handyman who calls himself a clog wog and claims to have painted more than 4000 houses in Melbourne.

And one little thing, just in case you forgot, you didn't invent wog humor. It was Simon Palomares and George

Kapiniaris who came up with the Tibaldi Brothers routine. They went to Foster Gracie to do multicultural comedy, and that's where you came in. And you know what? Simon and George are not half as successful in monetary terms as you are, but they just seem much, much happier.

You are talented, funny, handsome and smart, Nick, but you really give everyone the S. And you've made your point. Set an example. Please show us that you are humble too, and generous. Let us be proud of you. You are the Daryl Somers of wogs. Like him, you take everything far too seriously. Where's your sense of humour?

What gives me the qualification to talk about discrimination and the power of language? I'm a financially independent, loudmouthed, overweight woman with a brain from a poor family. To quote Sharon Stone: "A vagina and an opinion is a deadly combination."

Darling, you are a success. Relax.

Chris Lilley

Repeat after me: Chris Lilley is a genius, Chris Lilley is a genius, Chris Lilley is a genius. I've watched the first two episodes of his new mockumentary *Summer Heights High* twice just to make sure. I'm going to put my coke on the bloke here and say that *Summer Heights High* is a masterpiece. Think Ricky Gervais. Think Barry Humphries. Think the team behind *Kath & Kim*. At times I despair about the state of Australian television comedy. Then I think of Chris Lilley and I have more than hope. I'm excited.

You may be familiar with Lilley from the award-winning *We Can Be Heroes*. He wrote it, co-produced it and played five different characters. Enough of the over-achieving already! After watching *We Can Be Heroes*, I thought, "The guy can act his arse off and he's Captain Ideas Pants, but he's going to have to make a pretty big leap as a writer to pull off whatever's next." And guess what? He has. Congratulations, Mr Lilley.

In *Summer Heights High* Lilley has done pretty much everything apart from the catering. His performances are startling. You don't think, "There's Chris Lilley pretending to be someone else." He is someone else.

We're talking characters not caricatures. Which is rarer in Australian comedy on both telly and the big screen than a sighting of Peter Costello.

The writing is funny as. But layered too. The day after watching I found myself laughing at the funny lines but also thinking about the deeper social observations in the show. The show is set in a government high school and stars Ja'mie, the annoying and pretentious private-school girl we met on *We Can Be Heroes.* There's also Mr G, the deluded, bitter, power-hungry drama teacher who first appeared on *Big Bite*, and a new character, Jonah Takalua. He's a Tongan drop-out who is on his third school in 18 months after setting a student's locker alight at one school and spray-painting a dick and balls on the principal's car at another.

The peripheral characters are played so straight you have to keep reminding yourself that it's a mocko and not a doco. The casting is inspired.

Summer Heights High is such a standout because of its strong, creative vision and control. Lilley is probably a bit of a control freak, and that's a good thing. He needs to be. He'll only have this level of creative control if he stays at the

ABC. Or at least stays there long enough to have the clout of *Kath & Kim.*

Part of the ABC's charter is to develop talent. Which is one of the reasons I love watching the ABC. I watch the ABC because I want to. The other stations I watch because I have to. Apart from SBS. I watch that for the porn. "Why is that man having sex with the donkey during the news, Mummy?" "Because it's SBS, darling."

Take a bow, Chris Lilley. And don't go over to the commercial stations. Not yet anyway.

The Logies I

If you enjoy watching celebrities eat their own vomit, tune in on Sunday night to watch the Logies. Television's night of nights is four hours of nauseating, self-congratulatory toss that is so hilarious you can't help being reminded of the Commonwealth Games.

You're going to do it. I know you are going to switch over to see the vacuous scrags from *Neighbours* and *Home and Away* grin like idiots and laugh like drains as they love themselves stupid down the red carpet.

My personal favourites are the overpaid, overstayed, overlaid executives trapped in 1985. If only I could take you to the after-party. There you could witness young hopefuls, both female and male, eagerly hair-flick, ego-stroke and dry-hump these filthy, morally derelict embarrassments for the chance of a hosting job on *Totally Wild.*

Sunday night's awards promise to be no less cringy, provincial and tragic than the previous 46, despite the new Graham Kennedy Award for Most Outstanding New

Talent. Half of the awards are now peer-voted; they are the awards with the word "outstanding" in the titles. The ones voted by 14-year-old girls are those with the word "popular" in the title. For example, "Most Popular Airhead in a Pile of Shit."

It would be easy to bag the Logies. Goodness knows, I think I just did. But it's the spirit of the night that I enjoy. The delicious hypocrisy that is the nature of domestic awards is the whole "I think awards are crap" unless, of course, they win, then they are crying and thanking God faster than you can say "she has so had work done."

It's fitting to see stunning SBS documentaries and ABC public-affairs shows recognised apart from the fact that it's alongside programs such as *Big Brother 5* and *Deal or No Deal.* Don't get me wrong, I enjoy some of these shows, I just don't think that we should celebrate them.

I always look forward to the "overseas star" from the big wide world patting us on the head and telling us that we exist just before being asked what they think of Australia. I'd love to hear one say, "Well, from what I have seen, this industry is a depressing ghetto of nubile, brainless morons whose only talents are reading an autocue and growing hair. Where is my bag of cocaine, my massive cheque and that 16-year-old girl who wants acting lessons?"

It is worth mentioning that *Play School* is the 2006 Logies Hall of Fame inductee. Let's honour *Play School* by all means, but what does it say about our industry when only one woman has been inducted into the Hall of Fame yet the whole of Ramsay Street has? What next? Big Ted nominated for the Gold Logie? But, let's face it, he'd have a better chance of winning than John Wood.

What would I like to see? Catriona Rowntree dragged

behind a ute by her pubic hair, but I think that's just me. But they won't print that.*

Do we need the Logies? No. But God, they are fun and I wouldn't miss them for the world.

---

* And they didn't: they went with "the cast of 60 Minutes playing 'greasy pig' on an oiled-up stage." This was my wish-list of alternatives:

What would I like to see?

- A mud wrestle between Liz Hayes and Kerri-Anne Kennerly, refereed by a nude Maria Venuti.
- The nominees for Best New Talent to settle it in a cage fight.
- Daryl Somers to spontaneously combust.
- The cast of *Home and Away* to form a nude human pyramid, helped along by 3 kilos of Nutella.
- Ray Martin getting a back, crack and sack wax live on stage.
- Hi-5 being boiled alive by the fat they have had sucked off their faces.

The Logies II

Despite writing last year, "If you enjoy watching celebrities eat their own vomit, tune in on Sunday night to watch the Logies," and then describing television's night of nights as "four hours of nauseating self-congratulatory wank," I was offered a job writing on this year's Logies.

So my advice to writers is: do shit where you eat.

For people familiar with my writing, which relies heavily

on crude generalisations, involuntary swearing and my motto "Go in swinging," don't get too excited. I can assure you that this year's Logies will be the safest in living memory.

Television executives employ clever, creative people brimming with passion and say, "We love your work. Just make it safe and fun." Then they dilute the creatives. Which in turn dilutes us all.

As a television viewer, television writer and television reviewer, being asked to write for television's best and fairest pie-night *is* like being asked to eat your own vomit.

I have written for the Logies, the ARIAs and, most hilariously, the 2005 AFI awards for Russell Crowe. I love award shows. It's like watching a tightrope walker. Half of me hopes they get to the other side safely, and the other half is rooting for them to plummet to their death.

So back to the Logies. Or as the "international stars" here to plug their latest cry for help or resuscitate their flagging careers call them, the Lergies, Lodgies or Looggies. Their appearance is meant to make us feel that we have a vibrant and exciting industry that the rest of the world aspires to. It isn't and they don't.

The show is sponsored by *TV Week*, a magazine read by people who think that *Home and Away* is a documentary. The awards fall into two categories. The Most Popular awards are voted by 14-year-old girls with mobile phones. The Most Outstanding awards are peer-voted. There is not one single nomination that appears in both categories.

This is how planning for such a show goes. Six weeks out there are loads of great ideas that promise to make the show the most exciting and memorable ever. Sketches and stunts come up such as having the casts from *Neighbours* and *Home and Away* in a scrag-fight. Other ideas are thrown around:

video packages of the nominees taking the piss out of television; how to control the boys from *The Chaser*; and suggestions about how to convince Eddie to do something. Anything. Producers generally use words such as "new," "fresh" and "edgy." Everyone's excited.

About three weeks in, the wheels fall off as celebrities pull out of anything considered funny, irreverent, edgy or all of the above. They think about it too much and get scared. Or their pimp, sorry, I mean manager, decides that it won't help their career to appear to have a sense of humour and a healthy disrespect for the industry. Which is hilarious when you realise that many of these rising stars have a use-by date of three months and will probably be seen at next year's Logies serving the guests drinks. That's if they are not in rehab or recovering from a vaginoplasty.

Suddenly footage is unavailable, network execs are scared of "burning people" and the last three weeks are spent cobbling up an awards show that can only be described as "not as bad as we thought." The nominees and presenters who have agreed to scripts suddenly get bored or scared, want more alternatives, then end up coming up with their own stuff. And if it doesn't work, they blame the writers. The producers will then lament that they probably shouldn't have given "the talent" the script, just told them what to do on the day in order to "get wood."

Knowing this means that you try not to give out all the lollies at the start of the trip. You see, if you give them all the best lines a month before showtime comes around, they'll be "over them" because they've heard the lines hundreds of times. They forget that the audience hasn't. So you need to keep something up your sleeve. I suggest cocaine and a Maurie Fields joke book.

The Logies, and indeed all commercial television, is like dealing with a three-year-old in a cot. They want every single toy in with them just so they can throw them all out then scream for something new. Which they then throw at your face. They tell you that even though they liked that thing yesterday, they don't like it now. Because it's not new.

Television is about quantity and not quality. When handing in scripts you're always trying to go right to the edge but not over it. Because if they pick out one little something too racy, too expensive or too "out there," they'll pull the pin on the whole thing instead of working the idea, no matter how brilliant the idea is. But you never know where that edge is, because it keeps shifting. I've seen writers floor a meeting with a genius idea and then a week later you ask about the idea and "Oh, we've had second thoughts and we don't think it will work." During this process the fine people who actually work on the show almost die from stress, exhaustion, lack of sleep and self-medication through alcohol. The writers, editors, producers and directors are dedicated, devoted and expert at what they do. Even people from overseas say that.

And I cannot stress how narrow-minded, gutless, sexist and bigoted your average studio executive is. These BWMs (Bogans With Money) are only one link in the food chain up from the creeps who run commercial radio.

The pre-taped video packages and sketches are written first and the obituary package is always done last. The writers sit in the writers' room flicking through magazines waiting for a list of stuff to write. You are given a brief of what to write and start cracking on it either alone or with another writer. It will be a friendly wrestle to come up with something that fits the brief. Good writers know their strengths and weaknesses and therefore know when to concede and when to push the line. The most important thing is to find the right voice for the task and the person who will be saying it.

It is well known that no one wants to host the Logies. Last year three presenters opened the show and this year they have three key presenters. If the show goes down like a lead balloon, no one wants to be known as the one flying it. The hosts or key presenters generally write their own stuff, often with their own writer. Occasionally the writers' room is asked to come up with some alternatives. These lines generally don't get up unless they are killers.

This year, while discussing the list of potential presenters, I said, "It's a bit light-on for women," to which people snapped back, "Well, it's the same as last year and no one complained." Any woman I mentioned was kyboshed with "not up to it," "divides the audience," "loose cannon" or "not in Melbourne." So look forward to about one female to every two males on stage. And none who looks over 35.

You know those, "I'm sorry I can't be with you tonight but I'm thrilled to receive this award" schticks for the nominees abroad? All nominees tape them if possible. I always thought they told the winner beforehand and got them to do it. Not true. No one knows the winners until the last moment, not even the people who work on the show. They want to maintain the magic.

There is an enormous and ridiculous amount of cloak-and-dagger secrecy involved in television. And a massive amount of fear. Much of the stuff I have written in this article is considered secret but common knowledge to people in and out of the industry. While writing for the Logies I was constantly told, "You can't say that/write that/do that."

I'd reply, "Everyone knows, so why not?" Silence. Then, "You just can't."

No matter what a joke every single person in the industry thinks the Logies are, due to the tiny size of our industry we are forced to buy into this festival of mediocrity because an appearance, nomination or win can pay your rent. And a call from Eddie can convince even the most well-respected and highly regarded person in the industry to do almost anything.

So why am I writing on the show? I am a work slut. That's the thing with our tiny industry. Hopefully, if you just keep getting work, one day you'll end up getting your own project up or end up working on something brilliant.

The Logies are not a celebration of excellence; they are a bizarre reality show. The Popular awards diminish the recognition that the winners of the Outstanding awards deserve because they have worked hard, taken risks and listened to their hearts, not to demographics, focus groups and ratings.

RocKwiz

These days people talking to me no longer open up with "How are you?", "Have you been busy?" or "Are those your kids trying to set that cat alight?" They mostly start the conversation with, "So, who are you going to get stuck into this week?"

Answer? This week? No one. I waded through the current television landscape of mindless reality programs, stale crime series and hysterical current affairs and you know what? *RocKwiz* stood out like a stubby of Coopers Red in a bath full of Carlton Draught tinnies.

Hey Hey It's Saturday Night was the show you watched when you were 14 and wanted to go out but couldn't. SBS's *RocKwiz* is the grown-up version for those of us who can't be stuffed making the effort and couldn't fit into our old jeans even if we did.

RocKwiz is a top Saturday night without the hangover, the cost of babysitting and feeling tragic because you are, in fact, tragic as you start yawning at 10.05 pm.

Brian Nankervis has been a part of both shows, creating, producing and co-hosting *RocKwiz* and poncing around on *Hey Hey* as Raymond J. Bartholomew doing poems about pole-vaulters. Nankervis, television's most popular warm-up guy among other things, created this funky, intelligent music quiz-show and had the genius to cast Julia Zemiro as the sassy, witty and clever host. I like her so much I think that I'm in love with her.

The show is a music quiz set in a room in a pub. But not just any old room in any old pub – the seedy, glorious and infamous Gershwin Room at the Espy in St Kilda.

The look of the show is so perfectly Espy circa 1992 that I can't help feeling that I am wearing Poppy lipstick and a brown suede jacket that smells of Styvos and that I look like Julia Zemiro. Although the truth is that I am in my pyjamas, on the couch eating some leftover shepherd's pie, and I actually look more like Nankervis.

The feat of creating this kind of effortless, laid-back entertainment is incredibly difficult. The fact that Nankervis and his team of television practitioners and musicians are able to translate the feeling of live music in a pub into television is a testament to the passion and care used to create this great show.

Now in its third season, the quiz consists of two teams of

three people. Four music nerds selected from the audience and two mystery music guests who perform a duet to finish the show. The guests are usually people like The Guy From The Hoodoo Gurus, That Girl Who Used To Be In The Clouds and I Can't Remember Her Name But She's Woody Guthrie's Daughter. Tune in tonight and check out That Irish Bloke From The Hothouse Flowers and That Bird From Fairground Attraction. Enjoy the blasts from the past and sing along if you know the words.

It's enough to make you want to turn off the telly, get your albums out, turn the stereo up and party on.

But whatever you do, don't leave the couch.

The Melbourne Comedy Festival

I am proudly un-Australian. The whole sport, barbie, tanned, blonde and beachy business was never really me. For a while I identified more with my Irish heritage. It seemed a better fit: loud-mouthed, wide-hipped, total disrespect for authority, love a good yarn and a plate of spuds. All with bad teeth.

But these days, I know what I am. I am a Melburnian to the core. If I wasn't born here, I would have moved here.

I love Melbourne. Which doesn't mean I can't love anywhere else. I'm with Samuel Johnson: "Patriotism is the last refuge of a scoundrel." I adore the breathtaking glittering city of Sydney, and Tasmania is one of the most beautiful places that I have ever been. When I was in a plane on my way to Port Douglas a few years back, I spoke to people from Los Angeles who had been travelling for more than 24 hours. I said to them, "I promise, it's worth it." And it was.

The mercurial Melbourne weather allows you to wear all the clothes in your wardrobe and eat all the food you love. Melburnians are informed, opinionated, love a good feed and are always up for a chat, or a stoush. This time of year is particularly intoxicating. Blue skies, cool nights, clothes drying quickly but warm stuff in your belly for dinner and the kids in bed early. I wake up in Melbourne, but feel as if I have died and gone to heaven.

It's the Melbourne International Comedy Festival. I really, really love the Melbourne Comedy Festival. And no, I have not been asked to write something on the festival because the *Age* is a sponsor. I write compelled by love or truth. If I could be bought, I'd be turning tricks for advertising.

When I get my hot little hands on the festival program, my heart starts pumping as I go nuts with the red pen and the Post-It notes. I then sink as much as I can afford on tickets and babysitters. Then it's counting down the sleeps and it's on with the boots, tights, scarf and red lipstick and down to the Melbourne Town Hall. This dull, soulless building is transformed into an exhilarating, vibrant palace brimming with people queueing, blabbing in the bar or hanging round the coffee wagon waiting for their caffe lattes. Listen and you will hear every other person say: "This is amazing. Is it always like this?"

The whole experience is life-affirming and glorious. And the festival is like a drug; maybe it's more like gambling, as I promise myself: "OK, just one more show." People accost friends between shows with "What have you seen? When are they on? You've got to see him/her/them."

The beauty of this festival is that it is accessible and it's cheap. Some shows feel like a fun night out with mates, while others drag you abruptly out of your comfort zone.

And others are crap and you slag them off on the way home. Which is all part of the experience. Watching the audience is almost as much fun as the show. You'll see all types: bogans, old folks, ladies from Malvern, goths, students, pimply teens and suburban mums and dads all hoping for something to make their hearts sing.

So far I have seen 14 shows and have about the same number to go.

Men of Steel is a top pick. I took my kids (five and nine) and they laughed like drains. It's not specifically a kids' show, it's an anyone show. Good, clean fun. And that's from someone who considers swearing and debauchery a hobby.

For those of you who don't think chicks are funny, check out *D-Cuppetry* (*Puppetry of the Penis* with tits) and Josie Long's homemade, heartfelt, very funny show. Or better still check out more than 20 lady comedians at Upfront13 next Tuesday. All Girls. All Live. All Funny.

My best find so far is Phil Nicol, a man described as "a mentalist." If you miss the late Bill Hicks and the late John Herouvim and you love hard-core, in-your-face comedy then check out Phil's show, *The Naked Racist*. I went twice in two days. The word on the street is that if you liked Phil Nicol you'll love *We Are Klang*.

And whatever you do, don't miss *Keating!*.

And, of course, there's Daniel Kitson. I saw him for the first time a few years back and he said something along the lines of "don't be alarmed that I dress like a child molester." I saw him last week at a secret midnight show at Trades Hall and got home at 3 am. He is one of the most astonishing comic talents of our time.

See something. Anything. Book a night. Do three shows.

I'll babysit for you. Don't turn around and say "I meant to go." There's plenty of time to sleep when you're dead.

Wilfred

I had a plasterer do some work at my place a while back. His name was Possum. Eats, roots and leaves, apparently. I was wrong; I thought they called him Possum because he ate food out of rubbish bins and smelt like road kill. Anyway, Poss and I got talking.

"So I hear you 'kin write for 'kin telly 'n' that."

"That's right, Poss."

"Well 'kin, next time you're in at 'kin Channel Nine 'n' that, tell 'kin Brian Naylor or 'kin whatever his 'kin name is to put 'kin Paul Hogan Show back on, will ya? That was 'kin piss funny that was. 'Kin takin' the piss out of wogs 'n' sheilas and that. Better than the 'kin shit they've got on these days."

As you can see, people are constantly moaning about the state of Australian comedy. "Why can't we make stuff like *Extras*, *The Office*, *The Daily Show*, *Curb Your Enthusiasm*, *Seinfeld*?" they ask.

First, let me assure you that the UK and the US churn out plenty of crap too.

Secondly, most television executives are not only gutless but they think they are creative when they are just blokes in suits. And very good at being blokes in suits. They think what they have is vision, when what they actually have is a big office and a massive boner with their secretary's name on it.

If you are a telly executive, repeat after me: "I give the

creatives creative control. And everything will be just fine. I am a television executive because I am not creative. I play golf and my favourite band is Fleetwood Mac."

Thirdly, good news. There is fresh, new ball-tearing Aussie comedy in just a few sleeps. It is short on chicks, but we'll unpack that in another column.

If you have often despaired at the absence on TV of bong-smoking dogs that think they are human, despair no more. *Wilfred* is a new comedy on SBS about, you guessed it, a bong-smoking dog who thinks he's human. Who says that SBS stands for Sex and Bloody Soccer?

Jason Gann and Adam Zwar (gifted performers from *The Wedge*, but don't hold that against them) wrote and performed *Wilfred* the short film and have developed it into a series. It's a solidly written, extremely well-acted cross between the creepiness and the weirdness of *League of Gentlemen* and *Spot the Dog*. It is the kind of show that you'd look at and ask: "Why can't we make stuff like this in Australia?"

Well guess what? We just did.

But wait. There's more! *The Chaser's War on Everything* is also returning in a shiny new timeslot.

I adore those boys. Brave, irreverent, smart, funny mavericks each and every one. They're not always right, occasionally they are very wrong, but that's what makes it so right. They're edgy, provocative, rough round the edges, in-your-face and no one could accuse them of being biased. *The Chaser*'s war really is on everything. And they prove that it costs just as much to make bad television as it does to make great television.

Politics

*

John Howard

What set out to be a pleasant lunch went horribly wrong. A mate who's always right about these things said, "John Howard's going to win the next election and I'll put money on it, can you pass the salt?" Just like that. As resigned and despondent as a man on death row. Is there a sentence in the English language more chilling than that? And what's with the salt? To pour on the wound he just ripped open?

"NNNNNNOOOOOO!" I screamed. "No, he can't. I still can't believe that he won in 1996. He can't. Tell me that you're joking. Seriously. Stop mucking around. You're freaking me out. I'm leaving unless you tell me that you're just trying to freak me out. I'm getting my bag. Seriously. I'm walking out. This is me walking." He said nothing. Just sat there eating his soup looking sad.

Later that evening as I was researching the possibility of moving to somewhere more progressive, like Saudi Arabia, I realised that he was right. John Howard is going to win the next election. As skilfully as a well-organised cult, he has brainwashed middle Australia to be stupid, suspicious and scared. He's stunted imagination, originality and thinking and tried to cut us off from the outside world. He's a tiny man. He's short-sighted, small minded and has aspirational Australia eating out of his sweaty little hand.

Howard has raped industrial relations and turned workplace conditions back 100 years. Our children and our grandchildren will never be able to claw back the rights and the privileges that this man has snatched, wrestled and stolen from us. He has chosen to leave a legacy of individual wealth for the few over the benefits of a mature country where vision, compassion and justice breed equality and bounty.

Mandatory detention of refugees, the war in Iraq, *Tampa*, the children overboard, the decimation of Medicare, privatisation of education by stealth, the gutting of government schools ... the hits just keep on coming. But of all the disgraces, and there have been so many, his flat-earth attitude to the environment is the jewel in his "short way round but the long way home" philosophy. What has Howard done about the climate change crisis? Stuck his fingers in his ears and said, "I'm not listening I'm not listening."

How will history judge this small-town boy who should be running a newsagency, not a nation? I wonder what Howard's grandchildren will make of him as they fight each other for the last glass of water? I wonder if they will think of him as a murderer, a liar, a war criminal and an environmental and cultural vandal?

He's not bumbling Mr Magoo. He's as shrewd and cunning as a shithouse rat. Howard mines every opportunity for his own gain. "Drugs, terrorism, the abuse of Aboriginal children ... hmmmm, how can I make that work for me? National identity, national security, mateship, lucky country, fair go. Throw a few of those into the speech. The punters love that kind of gear. Drink beer? If I have to."

If Howard were a visionary and a great leader, his journey would be one of the greatest political legends of all time. In 1995, when Downer resigned and Costello didn't want the job, it was a case of "Well, every kid should get a kick of the footy." What tenacity. Time and time again Howard was passed over. But he kept putting his hand up. Inside his head saying "I think I can, I think I can." And did. He turned Australia into the dreamtime of his parents.

"Have a baby? Here's $4000." Don't pork-barrel me, you slimy bastard. Carpet my kid's classroom instead.

I hate that Howard is a brilliant politician. It's like calling Hitler a genius. But he is a brilliant politician. The xenophobes, the bullies, the scared, the insecure and the greedy just love him. "Me house is paid off, so's me ute. And me boat ... I'm alright Jack. That Little John Howard is all right by me. Better the devil you know."

But hang on. This guy *is* Satan.

Every time I see a picture of Howard with Bush I feel as if I'm in a pizza parlour looking at a wall of photos with the owner standing next to Rex Hunt, Rosemary Margan and Steve Jacobs. "Look, You can trust me. 'Cause I know famous people and they know me." Is Australia so comfortable that it can't be fagged? Not even one assassination attempt? Everyone's just got to the point that they think, "He's going to have to die eventually." I'm not so sure. He's still putting on that green and gold tracksuit and heading out every morning at a cracking pace. He'll be round for a while. And I'll put money on it too.

Paul Keating

Over the Labour Day weekend here in my home town, the People's Republic Of Moreland, the chat was not about the loss to the ALP's frontbench of our sitting member, Kelvin Thomson, after giving Tony Mokbel the thumbs-up. Nor was it about Big Kev's popularity going off like a frog in a sock. The BBQs, the supermarket queues and the sleepover pick-ups were still wall-to-wall people getting dewy-eyed about Citizen Paul's saunter through Australian politics last week.

Like many who have written in this paper and even more who have read it, I still feel as though I have bumped into an old flame and I'm having flashbacks to a passionate affair from my past. John Howard a "desiccated coconut"; Peter Costello "all tip and no iceberg." I wish I'd written that. I wish I'd said that. I flush with political and literary lust at the sheer genius of it. I miss him, too. Terribly.

I keep thinking about John Hewson jogging for hours and writing 50 pages of policy before breakfast while Keating was still swanning around in his dressing gown at noon, listening to Mahler. And when Hewson asked "Why won't you call an early election?", Keating said: "The answer is, mate, because I want to do you slowly." Magic.

I know he made some bad choices. I can never forgive him for sucking up to Soeharto despite the genocide in East Timor. But show me a politician who made no mistakes and I'll show you Gough Whitlam. Actually, hang on, whoops-a-daisy, East Timor again. Success in politics has as much to do with luck, vision and timing as it does with intelligence, knowledge and morals. Or lack thereof. But don't get me started on John Howard, I've got to be at a Christmas party in December.

Labor followers adore their leaders, unlike Liberal voters, who tolerate theirs. It has always struck me as hilarious how well Labor leaders' biographies sell in comparison to Liberal ones. A story on the *7.30 Report* a bit over a year ago pointed out that "John Howard, the most successful prime minister since Menzies – one book. Mark Latham, backbencher for most of his time in federal politics, failed Labor leader, six books – and, of course, his own political diaries."

I want a show with my dinner. But with Howard in charge there is no dinner, no show and dessert is David Hicks on toast. Keating sold the sizzle *and* the steak. Even if he did burn a few.

Keating described former National Party leader Ian Sinclair as "a political carcass with a coat and tie on," Malcolm Fraser as "like an Easter Island statue with an arse full of razor blades," and Hewson as "an abacus gone feral." But his stinging remarks were not reserved for the Coalition. And I'm not just talking about his comment that Brian Burke was smarter than two-thirds of the West Australian Labor Party rolled together. When Whitlam said "That was a good speech. You should go back, comrade, and get yourself an honours degree," Keating replied: "What for? Then I'd be like you."

How about "If you're not living in Sydney you are merely camping out"? So much for don't shit where you eat.

But it was at moments like the 1992 launch of the International Year of Indigenous Peoples that we fell in love with Keating: "It was we who did the dispossessing. We took the traditional lands and smashed the traditional way of life. We brought the diseases. The alcohol. We committed the murders. We took the children from their mothers. We practised discrimination and exclusion. It was our ignorance and our prejudice. And our failure to imagine these things being done to us."

People say that they make an informed choice. Crap. We barrack. Fickle swinging voters withhold their tragic little lollies like five-year-olds. "I haven't decided who I am going to give it to yet. It depends who is nicest to me."

Even if the Liberal Party promised me everything I wanted – free high-quality healthcare, child care and education, troops out of Iraq, George Bush's head on a stick, a pledge to no longer be environmental vandals and a slab and two pizzas delivered to my door every Friday – I still wouldn't vote for them because they are not my team.

If you are a fan, you must check out *Keating!*, "the musical we had to have." Watching Mike McLeish play Keating is like seeing a dead person.

I cringe as I watch Howard schmooze with powerful leaders and heads of state. I feel like a teenage punk when his dad picks him up from a party wearing a cardigan and slippers. Howard should be running a newsagency somewhere in the Bogan Belt, dreaming his parents' dreams instead of inflicting them on Australia.

Keating lost. He failed to capture the imagination of blue-collar Australia because blue-collar Australia has no imagination. And you can put that on my headstone.

Even Phillip Adams has called for Keating to re-enter politics. But the Labor Party would be mental to trot him out again. A few maverick cracks is one thing, but what we need now is Rudd and Gillard. Keating's time has past. And it's never coming back.

Kevin Rudd I

Let's be honest here, it's a bit hard to sex up Kevin Rudd. Sure, he's probably a good bloke. Actually, he must be a good bloke seeing that Howard and his mates have done their best to dig up dirt on him, and all they found out is that he speaks Chinese. The H-Team kept opening closets hoping skeletons would fall out and all they found were doilies, neatly folded linen and a tea towel that read "WANDILIGONG! IT'S ABORIGINAL FOR PARTY!"

I'm a bit obsessed with political slogans: *Incentivisation*, *It's Time* and *Ease the Squeeze* are all gold. When I am bored, I come up with my own. Howard: *Better the Devil*

You Know (Even if He's Satan). Rudd: *It's The Bubbles of Nothing that Make Him Really Something.* Labor: *I Can't Believe It's Not Liberal*; Liberals: *If You Liked Dad's Army, You'll Love the Liberals.*

When I first heard about Kevin07, I thought it was something cooked up by the boys from *The Chaser.* "The Name's Rudd. Kevin Rudd. Agent 07." But log on to kevin07.com and you'll find that Kevin Rudd is so down with the youth, he's practically an Emo. It's all YouTube, MySpace and Facebook. You can even sign up to KMAIL.

It's at this point that I have to make it clear that I am not joking. The only reason I feel the need to tell you that I'm not joking is because it sounds so far-fetched. Once upon a time politicians had policies, now they have blogs. I've been onto Kevin Rudd's Facebook profile – he has more than 5000 Facebook friends. Including me, and I can't stop poking him. I know, it's fully sick.

I can just hear Kev: "This whole Facebook thing. I don't know. It's not really me." "Don't worry about it Kev, do you think Howard likes drinking beer?"

You can hop onto Kevin07 and buy the gear. How's that for funky? Calling it "gear," not T-shirts. They must really understand the complex pressures of youth if they call it gear. So I clicked on gear, was transferred to ALP donations and bought a couple of T-shirts. I'll be keeping them in mint condition with my VOTE YES FOR AN AUSTRALIAN REPUBLIC windcheater.

Zip over to Kev's MySpace page and you'll find that he's got 13,374 friends. I had a good squiz and now I know heaps more about what Kevin Rudd has to offer, which means that I still know pretty much bugger-all. But it all sounds good. Kev doesn't need to try though, he'll be getting my vote, but not my primary. The Greens will be getting my $2.10 for electoral funding. I don't believe in the secret ballot, I believe we should all have who we vote for tattooed on our foreheads, so when we're at parties we know where to go for a good rant, and where to go to punch someone's head in.

I decided to check out if John Howard has a MySpace page. He does, and he has 14,604 friends. George Bush, Alexander Downer, Peter Costello, John "True Blue" Williamson and *The Chaser's War on Everything*. Here is a sample of the more polite comments from John Howard's "friends": "GO ROT IN HELL"; "Pass the bong"; "How about addressing gay rights, you pig?"; "Get your eyebrows waxed"; "make my babies"; "i dnt get it r u labour or libral?"

But hang on here. Peter Costello, a friend? Sounds a bit dodgy. I started snooping and my instincts were right. It seems the John Howard MySpace page is NOT official. The Liberal Party of Australia has nine friends, according to myspace.com/howardgovernment. Surprise, surprise, it's not official either. But your average MySpace surfer wouldn't know because they wouldn't check. What's real in the cyber world? Who knows? But it sure quacked like a duck.

This must be a little awkward for Howard's image manipulators. Will the strong and official presence of Kevin Rudd online force the Howard administration to give in? To go against their straighty-one-eighty image and get down and funky with the cyber dudes simply to look as "cool"? Which they won't. If it doesn't hook into the online community, the Coalition could do itself some serious damage at the ballot box. By getting "down with the youth," Kevin Rudd may get the John So He's My Bro cute-cult-nerd vote. Keep in mind that an email campaign is responsible for the fact that 71,000 Australians ticked their religion as Jedi in the last census. I was one of them.

When I first started checking out Kevin07, I was amused. But I can't help wondering if it's dumbing down or simplifying? Either way, it's a good laugh. And quite nice T-shirts. Got to go and poke Kevin.

Kevin Rudd II

Last week my column began with the line: "Let's be honest here, it's a bit hard to sex up Kevin Rudd."

Well guess what? Consider Big Kev officially sexed. The spin doctors couldn't do it. Kev himself wouldn't do it. But the people who shouldn't have done it did it.

A big hello to Alexander Downer and the Liberal Party Dirt Unit if you are reading this! And a big thank you from all of us here who are gagging to see the back of John Howard. Suddenly, it seems that dreams really can come true. Keep up the good work.

How much do I love desperate politics? In an attempt to dig up dirt on Big Kev, what the dirt-diggers have actually done is found gold for Kevin07. They've kicked a goal for the other team. In one fell swoop and seven sweet words, "KEVIN RUDD WENT TO A STRIP JOINT," Rudd's popularity will go off like a frog in a sock. Suddenly The Politician Formally Known as the Best We Can Do is one of us. Big Kev got drunk and did something stupid.

Well, guess what? Haven't we all? Except, of course, John Howard. Don't be surprised if, when the Coalition gets a whiff of what a positive impact this has on Rudd's credibility, they set up Howard with a bottle of Blue Nun, a nude lady and a bar called Hot and Horny.

Kevin Rudd was overseas for work, got drunk and ended up in a strip bar. You say that like it's a bad thing. Alexander Downer is officially a bigger dickhead than I originally thought. How out of touch is the bastard son of the squattocracy with the average voter if he thinks that by revealing Rudd once got drunk and ended up in a strip bar that we'll shake our heads, turn our backs and vote for Howard?

Every man has seen a stripper. Every man has looked at porn. Every man knows this. Women will be all, "Oh no, not my husband, father, son, brother." Wrong. They've all done it. Don't we want a leader who has lived a little?

Downer has made a few unsuccessful but hilarious attempts at making himself appear "an average bloke" in the past. Who could forget him in fish-nets and stilettos? Who wished they could? And how about him belting out a bit of karaoke at the end of the ASEAN conference all in the name of "I am not Little Lord Fauntleroy"? Australians have a finely tuned try-hard detector. And it went mental. Downer's biggest mistake was his attempt to come across as a comedian around the time of the Liberal Party slogan "The Things that Matter," joking that the party's domestic violence policy would be called the "things that batter." I can't imagine what the name of the Downer biography will be. Maybe "What Was I Thinking?"

Aussies love sinners. This strip-club revelation will make your average voter think that Rudd may appear a bit uptight, but at least he is not "up himself." Because being "up yourself" is the worst thing anyone could ever call an Australian. Other than calling them a New Zealander. Aussies hate wowsers and are highly suspicious of people who won't join in the shout. The only thing worse is if they judge those who do: "Unlike you, I don't need to drink to have a good time."

Bob Hawke's beer-drinking and public displays of emotion had him labelled "a good bloke." We only warmed to Malcolm Fraser when he was found dazed and sans pants in a Memphis hotel lobby. Bill Clinton's "I did not have sexual relations with that woman" and "I didn't inhale" made us think, "Legend!" If politicians appear too squeaky, we can't help thinking: "What are they hiding?" I'd be happy with: "Hello. I smoke, I drink, I have a tattoo and $5000 in parking fines. Vote for me."

Australian voters don't mind sinners, but they won't tolerate hypocrites. A bit of wayward behaviour from their politicians is fine as long as it doesn't contradict their policies.

Rudd told his wife at the time. That's what matters to me. And that's the only thing that's important. Marie Coleman, spokeswoman for the National Foundation for Australian Women, said it appeared Rudd had been "pissed as a newt," which didn't excuse his behaviour but meant it was reasonable to give him the benefit of the doubt that it was out of character. But at the same time, the odd act that is "out of character" is integral to the Australian character. And the human condition.

If I want dirt, I'll watch *Backyard Blitz*. Voters don't want taxpayers' money funding witch-hunts. Voters don't want "I know you are, but what am I?" Voters want policies. Voters want solutions. Voters want ideas. Sure, it hit the fan, but it flew straight back into the Liberals' faces. Liberal Dirt Unit? You're soaking in it.

Election 2007

At a chicks' dinner on Friday night we all watched the footy. I'm not that into sport. Politics is more my cup of blood. But I do enjoy a good stoush, and Friday night's game between Collingwood and one of those newfangled teams not from Victoria was a pearler, with the Pies winning in a nail-biter.

I've been getting just as excited about the election. And I'm not alone. Folks who don't usually want to chat about politics are engaged. Mates who normally drag themselves off to vote telling anyone who will listen that "they're all crooks anyway" are keen to talk. Not just in a footy tipping kind of way but seriously discussing the issues. WorkChoices, climate change, the price of living, the war in Iraq, the funding of schools, a revamp of public health. It's not just about Labor versus the Coalition or Howard versus Rudd – there is a real feeling that it's time for a new direction.

And Bennelong. Never in the history of Australian politics has anyone cared so much about what happens in one seat. Eden-Monaro? Couldn't give a monkey's. But how will we feel if Maxine McKew pulls it off on election night? It gives me goosebumps just thinking about it.

I keep imagining myself on election night, threading pieces of kabana and pickled onions onto toothpicks and poking them into oranges, sick to the stomach with excitement about a night in front of the telly with Antony Green and Kerry O'Brien. A cliffhanger result now seems unlikely as John Howard appears content to stone himself to death. Remember when John Hewson asked Paul Keating why he wasn't calling an election and Keating replied, "Because I want to do you slowly"? Well, it seems that Howard is doing himself slowly.

If I were John Howard, I'd be praying for a terrorist attack. Or a heart attack. If I were him, I'd rather that than give in. We've all watched Beattie, Bracks and Thwaites know when their time is up. Howard is coming across as selfish, mad with power and refusing to listen to what's best for his party. Or the country.

There was a great interview about the leadership on the *7.30 Report* last week. Howard banged on about his commitment to the job and his party's loyalty to him. This after Downer held a leadership discussion without Peter "Strap on the Fake Smile" Costello. Howard's interview was peppered with words like vision, future and energy. Terms like "the honest truth," "I love the job," "If the Australian public are good enough, kind enough to re-elect me" and "I'm asking for the public to vote for someone who levels with them." Then Kerry O'Brien asked about the potential negative for the voters in Bennelong of voting in someone who will be retiring mid-term.

John Howard: "Well the question … well … well … well … the … the … the position in the position in relation to that is … I mean I'm very, very upfront, I mean whether depending on when I went whether there'd be a by-election or not is something that I would determine then because … um … it has not been unknown for people in those circumstances to serve out their term and it would depend entirely on circumstances."

Weasel words. That's all we are getting at the moment. No policies, no vision, no commitments. Just weasel words.

The angry and disillusioned are hoping for a grudge match come election night. It's not enough for the Howard government to be voted out. People want to see blood. They want to see Howard cockily strutting into the election claiming smugly, "We are the underdog" – a sure-fire sign that a party thinks they've got it in the bag – only for it to go horribly wrong as the votes come in.

Costello won't challenge for the job and Howard is like a dog with a bone. I'll put money on Malcolm Turnbull throwing his hat in the leadership ring. Which would be a welcome distraction from watching the Liberals going the thump on each other.

Voters don't want Labor to get in simply because the Liberals have lost the plot. We want great campaigns, inspired speeches, passionate debates, original ideas and a good fight. And oranges covered in toothpicks spiked with cheese, kabana and gherkin.

Citizenship Test

You can shove your citizenship test up your poxy date. No one has the right to decide what being Australian is. I was born here and I have no idea. But I do know what it isn't, and what being Australian isn't is testing people on what they know about some white pen-pusher's idea of Australia. This is the country whose citizens pride themselves on not knowing the words to their own country's anthem.

If I wanted to be an Australian citizen and I was told that I had to pass a test first, I'd bugger off to New Zealand.

Who are we trying to keep out with this test? How will knowing the name of Australia's first prime minister or the date of federation keep out terrorists, wankers or bludgers? The citizenship test questions are irrelevant and offensive.

Here's my citizenship test. And if you don't like it, you can rack off and go back to your own country. You know what the most un-Australian thing in the world is? Migrants. And we don't want them coming here with their fancy food, classy culture, rich traditions and willingness to contribute.

LANGUAGE

1. Do you understand the meaning, but are unable to explain the origin of, the term "died in the arse"?
2. What is a mole?
3. Are these terms related: chuck a sickie; chuck a spaz; chuck a U-ey?
4. Explain the following passage: "In the arvo last Chrissy the relos rocked up for a barbie, some bevvies and a few snags. After a bit of a Bex and a lie-down we opened the pressies, scoffed all the chockies, bickies and lollies. Then we drained a few tinnies and Mum did her block after Dad and Steve had a barney and a bit of biffo."

CUSTOMS

1. Macca, Chooka and Wanger are driving to Surfers in their Torana. If they are travelling at 100 km/h while listening to Barnsey, Farnsey and Acca Dacca, how many slabs will each person consume on average between flashing a brown eye and having a slash?
2. Complete the following sentences: a) If the van's rockin' don't bother … b) You're going home in the back of a … c) Fair suck of the …
3. I've had a gutful and I can't be fagged. Discuss.
4. Have you ever been on the giving or receiving end of a wedgie?
5. Do you have a friend or relative who has a car in their front yard "up on blocks"? Is his name Keith and does he have a wife called Cheryl?

FOOD

1. Does your family regularly eat a dish involving mincemeat, cabbage, curry powder and a packet of chicken noodle soup called either chow mein, chop suey or kai see ming?
2. What are the ingredients in a rissole?
3. Demonstrate the correct procedure for eating a Tim Tam.
4. Do you have an Aunty Myrna who is famous for her tuna mornay and other dishes involving a can of cream of celery soup?
5. In any two-hour period have you ever eaten three-bean salad, a chop and two serves of pav washed down with someone else's beer that has been nicked from a bath full of ice?
6. When you go to a bring-your-own-meat Barbie, can you eat other people's meat or are you only allowed to eat your own?
7. What purple root vegetable beginning with the letter "b" is required by law to be included in a hamburger with the lot?

CULTURE

1. Do you own or have you ever owned a lawn mower, a pair of thongs, an Esky or Ugg boots?
2. Is it possible to "prang a car" while doing "circle work"?
3. Who would you like to crack on to?
4. Who is the most Australian: Kevin "Bloody" Wilson, John "True Blue" Williamson, Kylie Minogue or Warnie?
5. Is there someone you are only mates with because they own a trailer or have a pool?
6. Would you love to have a beer with Duncan?

The people to be granted citizenship are the ones who call it a crock and cheat.

The Republic

Even if the Australian flag had a picture of a bloke called Davo chucking a brown eye on it or the image of a pav whipped up by Aunty Bev, I don't imagine that I could ever be a flag-waver. But at least if our country's flag did have these pictures, I'd be able to look at it and not feel like a 40-year-old still living at home with my parents.

Still being part of "The Empire" feels exactly like that. Like we are living at home with our parents. Despite attempting to delude ourselves that we are "world class," a "global leader," or part of the "axis of evil" – sorry, I mean "coalition of the willing" – we are a dole-bludging bong-head living out the back of our parents' place. (No offence to dole-bludging bong-heads living out the back of their parents' place.)

Even Prince Charles thinks that it's time we flew the coop. He's gone down to the bungalow, stormed in and said: "Are you still here? One thought one got one's arse into gear ages ago. One might consider pulling one's finger out and getting one's own life."

And what have we done? Sat there in our tracky-dacks and boxing kangaroo singlet, handed the spliff to our mate Knackers, picked up the PlayStation controller and said: "Can't be stuffed, mate."

Because we tried once. Didn't work out. So we just continue self-medicating with a couple of she'll-be-rights and a lie-down every arvo. "'Cause if it ain't broke mate ..." But it is. Australia is broke because it's never been fixed. It's never been assembled. It's still in the flat pack with the allen key.

Are the English going to have to chuck us out first? Are we that laidback? $100 says that England's going to be a republic before us. "Sorry chaps, we are selling the family home and buying a campervan. To use your term, 'You're rooted.'"

How embarrassing is it that we aren't a republic? I cringe when I meet folks from abroad and they realise that we are still part of the Commonwealth. I shrink when they ask why we have England's Queen on our coins, only for me to tell them that she's our Queen too. They're flabbergasted.

I have often wondered why the Queen can have the top job in Australia despite the fact that it defies our equal opportunity laws. "Yes, we proudly enforce our meritocracy and rules of equality ... apart from the boss lady because that's different."

So much for common wealth. The Queen's fortune was recently conservatively estimated to be about $US500 million ($A590 million) by *Forbes* magazine. Some suggest that it's closer to $US10 billion. Would it kill her to spread it round a bit?

I hate to admit it, but a recent trip to America had me envious of their flag. A flag they chose and were not allocated. They talk of their founding fathers, their war of independence and their coming of age. They made a decision. And they fought for it. East Timor has self-determination and we do not. What a scathing example of our apathy that is. How easy it would be for us. And how difficult it was for them.

Let me simplify this for you. We have a referendum. The

question is: Do you want us to be a republic? Tick the box. A) Yes B) No C) Let Me Ask My Husband.

Keep the Westminster system. Personally, I'd be happy with a benevolent socialist dictatorship, but that's what happens when you have a columnist from the People's Republic of Moreland.

As far as a president is concerned, I don't give a rat's about the process. The president could be Tony Mokbel's rug for all I care, just so long as we are a republic. And why do we need to call our head of state the president? How about something more Australian. Like "the Big Whoop." "Please Stand for the Big Whoop of the Republic of Australia. Shane Keith Warne ..."

What do we do about the Commonwealth Games? We change the name to the Piss-Weak Countries Who Have Bugger-all Chance of Winning at the Olympic Games. All those royal hospitals, royal societies, with your royal this and royal that? Change the word from "Royal" to "Bonzer," "Ripper" or "Beaut."

Being a republic will make a monumental difference to Australia. We will stop looking to other countries and look at ourselves. Our confidence will blossom, our dynamism will flourish and our imagination will run wild. Our originality will leave other countries thinking: "If they can do that, maybe so can we." And it will affect our daily lives.

It will break my heart if I don't die in the Republic of Australia.

The wide, wide world of TV

*

Australian Princess

You've got to love a show that begins like this: "Previously on *Australian Princess* [CUT TO PRESS CONFERENCE]...

"Is it true that you are a lesbian?"

"I heard you've got your nipples tattooed. Is that correct?"

[CUT TO THE QUEEN WALKING PAST THE GIRLS FROM *Australian Princess*.]

Her Maj: "I saw that on the television."

Are there any words in the English language less compatible than "Australian" and "princess"? Tuna-scented bath gel? Barbed-wire undies? Tony Abbott's warmth? Nope. They may be top chicks, beaut sheilas and cracking birds but these women are not Australian princesses. I should know, because I've watched five hours of this program and I hate myself for it.

As far as telly goes, the program is unoriginal but well executed. Twelve young women vie for the title of Australian Princess, judged by a panel of, well, people prepared to do anything to get their heads on the box. Paul Burrell, former royal servant (that classy bloke who wrote a tell-all book about his life as Princess Diana's butler). His best line so far? "King Henry VIII's second wife was not Anne of Green Gables." Jane Ferguson, the Duchess of York's sister, whose only claim to fame is looking like a camel. And Jean Broke-Smith, grooming and etiquette expert: "Amanda is a pretty girl but she's still too noisy for me."

The girls are, to put it mildly, a bunch of Aussie scrags. But I say that affectionately, because princesses are stuck-up wankers. We Australian women pride ourselves on our she'll-be-right, back-off-dickhead, get-your hand-off-it attitude.

Not on the way we cross our legs, drink our tea and nibble sandwiches. We neck bottles, scoff pizza and call a spade a fucking spade.

We've lost a few great girls already. Amanda the republican doctor who, when the Queen walked past, said, "She was so close I could have stuck out my foot and tripped her over." Leanne, who asked the judges, when they said she'd make a great politician's wife, "Why not a politician?" Gone too, Kate the pig farmer, who I adored, and Carla the bisexual goth.

But still in the running are Amy, who says bugger-all but looks like Princess Diana; Stephanie with the fake breasts, who said, "I've been told to be more sophisticated. I s'pose that means not hangin' me cans out"; and my favourite, Kylie Booby, the beauty therapist who dresses like a cheap Gold Coast hooker. When asked, "Are your boobs real?" she replied, "Yes they are. They're nice aren't they?"

Tune in this week for the second-to-last episode to hear, "I want to stick it to those other girls so badly it's not even funny. If they were standing on a street corner and it was legal I'd run them over"; a mention of toe jam; and "That stuff that comes out of snails' bums." But my favourite line of the show is: "Oh my god! They have cut out a cow's vagina and they've stuck it on my plate – and they're going to make me eat it!" Classy.

America's Next Top Model

America's Next Top Model is another "hopefuls from across the country vie for the coveted title of" show. Dime a dozen, I know. What grabbed my attention was not that it furnishes the viewers with an opportunity to witness attractive people make morons of themselves. And it wasn't because it was the first program that I have ever watched where I actually hated everyone in it.

What catapults this average show to excellence was its abundance of hilarious quotes. Every word is pure gold. *America's Next Top Model* is wall-to-wall, chock-a-block poetry.

Here's what the girls say about themselves: "I'm a fornicator, I'm a smoker and I'm a horrible example of what a Jehovah's Witness is supposed to be"; "Jewellery is like my main thing"; "I'm really girlie and I'm pretty pleased with that"; "I love getting dirty"; "You know how sociopaths can kill people and not feel bad about it? I'm like that except I never killed anybody"; "I'm a wild woman, I'm feeling the tree"; and "I can feel it going down my pants."

This is what they say about each other: "I am this close to hating her"; "What are you doing, you alcoholic bitch?"; "There's something weird about Lisa and I can't work out what it is"; "I love that you work at Dairy Queen, that's so awesome"; "She needs some sissyfication"; "She looks like a creature from I don't know where"; "I wish that I liked her"; "You were thinking a little too much on that photo shoot"; and "Are you a full-on lesbian?" To which the answer was: "Yes I am." And then they made out.

The opening credits promise "Fierce beauty, fabulous strut, fresh personality," but there's no mention of brains. Which may explain why one of the girls confidently proclaimed that all birds are blind.

America's Next Top Model does nothing to dispel the myth that beautiful people who get paid to wear clothes and walk around loving themselves sick for a living are vain, shallow and vacuous. Which is good.

Strap yourself in and listen to sentences that seem to be English but make absolutely no sense: "I want more face"; "I almost feel like the bubbles are owning you and you aren't owning the bubbles"; "You took a picture and you didn't rock it"; "Give me a big watermelon butt"; "Think pretty, but still scared"; "I'm just getting dead carcass on a fence right now"; "You've got beaten-up, bashed-up man fingers"; "She has pure seeing eyes"; "You're all looking sexified today"; and "I'm still losing your neck."

Sure, they're talking the talk but what's all this talk about walking? "Let's walk around and we'll see what we have to work with"; "I thought you were pretty boring with the walk"; and "It's amazing watching someone walk whose been walking for so long."

You have to hand it to these girls, total airheads each and every one, but they do give good face.

Pussycat Dolls

If you like moles, skanks and bitches you are probably already watching *Pussycat Dolls Present: The Search for the Next Doll.*

It's not so much life imitating art but more sluts imitation whores.

There's a band called the Pussycat Dolls. They are kind of like the Supremes, but the singers look like they turn tricks in primary-school car parks for cigarette butts. They sing that song "Don't you wish your girlfriend was hot like me? Don't you wish your girlfriend was a freak like me?" That's right, the tune they played at your grandparents' wedding. I'm familiar with the song because I'm trendy and down with the youf.

Familiar with the Backstreet Boys? Think Backalley Sallys. They are looking for another airhead, I mean artists, for their tribute to feminism. Hence the search to bring something new to the group. What? Like pubic lice. How proud would you be as a parent if your daughter was chosen? "John's an accountant, Kate's a teacher and Schapelle's a Pussycat Doll."

The Search for the Next Doll is in the same oeuvre as *Popstars* and *Australian Idol.* A stack of bright-eyed hopefuls get whittled, excruciatingly slowly, to a lucky one-hit wonder whose name no one will remember in three months. Their precious little dreams are shattered and smashed for our viewing pleasure.

The difference is that this show is a major scragfest. We are talking human Bratz dolls. The good, the bad and the ugly? Try the cheap, the tacky and the nasty. Sure, show a bit of leg and get those tits out for the lads by all means, but we're not going to Hobart, so there's no need to show us your map of Tassie.

The creator of the Pussycat Dolls, Robin Antin, features heavily in the show. She has the body of an 18-year-old, the head of a troll and a voice that could cut through corrugated iron. It seems that she has done for modern music what Stephen Hawking has done for theoretical physics. The idea of putting together a group of women dressed as slags, who sing songs that all sound the same is, apparently, not only groundbreaking but revolutionary.

The hopefuls get a makeover from Robin's brother Jonathan, who unlike his sister is very pretty, not that there's anything wrong with that. With the announcement of the makeover the girls squeal, jump up and down and almost go a bit lezzo with hugging. They rock down to Jonathan's boutique and Robin tells her brother that the girls have been "finding their persona from the inside and now it's time to rock their persona from the outside." Then it's high-fiving and whooping aplenty. Then Jonathan achieves the impossible and manages to turn the Pussycat Dolls into the Pussycat Dogs.

If you want to watch porn, watch porn. If you want to see music, switch to *Rage*. *The Search for the New Pussycat Doll* should only be viewed if you want to like, hear like, the word like, used like, 20 times in, like, every sentence.

Jack of All Trades

I love tradies. When they turn up. And when they do "rock up," they're usually late, fused to the mobile or have to rush off to another job. Which, by extension, must be either more important, better paid or involving a better-looking woman. Or involving a "lady" who has watched enough movies to know what etiquette is required when the tradie or pool cleaner "rocks up." [CUE BAD '80S GUITAR MUSIC].

I love the way tradies have nicknames such as Wombat, No Neck, Pineapple or Fing. And the way they enjoy their music loud and tuned slightly off the station. Don't get me wrong, I appreciate COCK ROCK FM as much as the next person. As long as the next person is John Howard's nana. The Eagles and Iron Maiden at 7.30 am really compliments the aroma of fried dim sims, Winfield Blues and a T-shirt that hasn't seen the inside of a washing machine since I was a size-8 blonde.

The first thing that you usually notice about a tradie is

that they are not there. If, by some miracle, they are, you will know by the ute parked outside your house with a bumper sticker that reads, "All you virgins, thanks for nuthin," or "Fat chicks shit me." Tradies are quite particular about their women, despite being not too fussy about their own personal hygiene.

Jack of All Trades is easy to miss. It's on just before the cricket. Which no one gives a flying monkey's about because we have already won the meat tray. Or whatever it is that they win. This show is a thinly veiled advertorial posing as a competition between tradies to be crowned King Gee Jack of All Trades. Ah the glory! First the tipping competition, then the skolling competition, now this! The competition involves tasks such as building a barbecue in 15 minutes and reversing a ute with a trailer attached between two portaloos.

This show is hilarious. Mostly because the tradies are in better shape than the cricketers but also due to its shameless product-placement. In one three-minute block they mentioned King Gee, Mitre 10, *Ralph*, Selleys, Crazy John and SsangYong. This show also allows you to sit back and enjoy the use of terms such as "game on," "do it once, do it right," "bring it on," "in the zone," "I am da man," "silent but violent" and "go hard or go home."

When tradies do turn up they are worth their weight in beer. Which they proceed to drink. From your fridge. They're happy to lift something for you as long as you don't mind being called "love" if you're a woman or "poofter" if you're a bloke. They are always quick with a joke, or 50 if they are "on fire." I particularly enjoy the predictable way that when shown what you want them to do, they suck air between their teeth, exhale dramatically, shake their head and announce, "Whoever done this last work should be shot."

I truly adore them. Give me a happy tradie over a bitter lawyer any day. *Jack of All Trades* promotes excellence in our tradies but I think they are pretty excellent already.

Age of Love

I wasn't going to write about *Age of Love*. I thought: a dating show starring Mark Philippoussis? If that's not boned in two weeks I'll do the macarena with Kerri-Anne.

I was wrong. It's still on. Curiosity got the better of me and I'm glad it did. Because I haven't had such a good laugh since my son asked me if I used to be a caveman.

OK, so Mark Philippoussis. Let me refresh your memory. Tall bloke, hair doesn't move, used to play tennis. Actually no, he used to play serve. Word on the street is that he did the nude thing with Paris while he was dating our Delta. Answers to Poo, body of a Greek god, brains of a doughnut.

Age of Love is one of those excruciating dating elimination shows; fancy digs, pash cam and industrial-strength sledging. Half the women are in their 40s and referred to as the cougars. The other half are in their 20s and called the kittens.

Are you cringing yet? Trust me, you will be.

My first thought was exactly the same as yours. Why would the Poo do this? For the cash? For the exposure? Then it dawned on me. For a root. If a tennis pro who owns a Lamborghini and has millions of dollars has to go to these lengths to get his end in, what chance is there for the rest of us? Apart from alcohol, pity and RSVP.com.

The Poo is a man known for dating chicks much younger than himself. Which makes the producer of this show a genius for initially presenting him with ten women over the age of 40 to choose to date.

When the first woman said: "I was born in 1967 and that makes me 41," the Poo strapped on the fake smile, clenched the jaw and swallowed hard. Then the rest teetered out ... 41, 43, 48. And when there were no more, he looked like a man forced to drink Adelaide tap-water for the rest of his life.

Now when I say 40, I'm not talking a 40-year-old woman who looks like, let me think, like me, for example.

I'm talking a 40-year-old who looks like one of the Veronicas. The fake breasts and tight faces? The cougars put them down to good genetics. Pants on fire.

So the Poo gets chatting with the old broads and he's surprised. A few dates with the lovely ladies and he's a new man. He's thinking Ashton and Demi, he's thinking Deborra-Lee and Hugh. That is until the new twist; ten 20-year-olds who also want a piece of the Poo.

They certainly impressed me with gems such as, "I'm young and definitely hot. Deal with it," "my dog's personality is just like mine" and "when guys see me on the street they're like 'she's really hot.'"

This exchange was gold:

Kitten: "I love food."

Poo: "Cool."

My favourite quote from the Poo so far was: "She looked hot, she looked hot. What can I say? She looked hot."

When the cougars meet the kittens, it's a scrag-fight, and it's on for young and old. And for us on the couch, top telly.

Chartbusting '80s

Growing up in the '80s knee-deep in *Punky Brewster*, *Diff'rent Strokes* and Choose Life T-shirts, I vividly remember being mortified at the musical cries for help that were the soundtrack of my youth. As I crimped my hair wearing khaki cord knickerbockers with metallic copper piping, the adults around me reminisced about being a teenager to the sounds of Bob Dylan, the Beatles, Velvet Underground, Joni Mitchell and Elvis. It then dawned on me that one day I would have to own up to being 16 and listening to Spandau Ballet, the Thompson Twins, Culture Club, Duran Duran and Cyndi Lauper. I was so deeply embarrassed that these were my coming-of-age anthems, I clearly remember thinking, "There is no way that the '80s are ever going to be fashionable again."

How wrong was I? I enjoy '80s music now far more now than I ever did during the '80s.

Which may explain why I love watching *Chartbusting '80s*. It's an '80s music video show with a live band, some old clips and a few '80s-inspired games. Sure, sounds unremarkable on paper but this show has been running for six years and is the highest rating show on Channel 31. It's clearly more than simply a good house in a bad street when you consider that it attracts about 100,000 viewers twice a week and the show has its third DVD coming out in October.

So what's its secret? A female host with the body of Sophia Loren, the mouth of a wharfie and more front than Myer. Josie Parelli hosts this show with Jeff Jenkins. Well she doesn't really host it, she takes over and mercilessly torments Jeff, or BR as she prefers to call him which stands for Bald Rodent. All between bad dancing, appalling singing and taunts such as, "You couldn't get a root with a fist full of 50s."

If I had three words to describe Josie I would use Bogan Wog Goddess. She prowls around the audience threatening to humiliate anyone who dares take her on in her '80s clothes and disco hair. And they love it.

The *Age*'s Jim Schembri, a longtime supporter of the show, had a go at her boogying during film clips and she retaliated by giving him a good spray on air saying that he was so low he would turn up at an Italian wedding with a gift of $20 sheets. She then introduced the Jim Schembri Dancers. That's chutzpah personified.

Tune in for the season's finale: two bands, two hours and two people who were married in the '80s who will renew their vows after sending in their what-was-I-thinking wedding photos.

Josie told me that the more profile she gets the more people suggest she lose weight, be submissive to Jeff and be less confronting if she wants to break into commercial TV. Fat chance. I was stunned when she told me that commercial TV had not approached her until I remembered that famous quote, "Women live in fear of men killing them and men live in fear of women laughing at them." Keep laughing, Josie.

Countdown

If you are between the ages of 30 and 50, have ever owned a pair of treads or can complete this lyric, "If I were a carpenter and you were a lady ..." you should watch The *Countdown Spectacular*. If you liked our rock stars when they were young and gorgeous, you will love them now they are middle-aged, chunky and gagging for a gig. They've gone from being hip to hip replacements and they've still got it. Just a bit slower.

Feel the nostalgia. Taste the remember-when. Put on your ah-the-good-old-days shirt to go with your that's-not-music-that's-noise-there's-no-tune pants.

We had film clips, the top ten and mumbling Molly, who, according to Wikipedia, is a former member of Mensa (note former). Throw in a bit of John Paul Young in satin pants, Renée Geyer and her flick-back hair, Mark Holden in a white suit and handing out carnations and Skyhooks in their glam-rock glory and you have a cultural revolution. And who could forget the state-of-the-art effect of opening the "Discovery" segment with the close-up of food colouring being squirted into a glass of water? Telly's all been downhill since then.

Here are some good reasons to watch tonight: Frankie J. Holden, Wilbur Wilde (you may recognise him from the Australian Pensioners Insurance Agency advertisements) and Ol' 55 belting out "On the Prowl"; Uncanny X-Men's Brian Mannix singing (I kid you not) "Everybody Wants To Work"; The Eurogliders; Cheetah (I must have been away that day); Leo Sayer with "When I Need You"; Les Gock from Hush looking like he has not aged in 30 years; Kids in the Kitchen; James Reyne performing "Reckless" in what appears to be a cravat; and Alex Smith from Moving Pictures looking more like Dick Smith as he sings "What About Me?" wearing glasses. And Sherbert. Howzat?

When Ross Wilson from Mondo Rock sang "Come Said The Boy" I had a violent flashback to the last time I heard that song and I was throwing up on a boy wearing a very skinny leather tie.

I could hang it on the ageing rock chicks with the words mutton and lamb or get stuck into the blokes' middle-aged spreads. But I can't because I just love them too much. These days the only drug they are taking is Mylanta and their biggest worry is how much can they earn and still get the pension. It's a night of top music with great sound and snappy editing. And how much do I love the audience? Soccer mums and blokes who work for the council feeling like they are 18 again and going right off. God bless 'em.

It's a magic 90 minutes but I did spare a thought for our dearly missed Shirley Strachan and Dragon's Marc Hunter.

The cultural impact of *Countdown* cannot be underestimated. Growing up with Enid Blyton, *The Flintstones*, the Queen on our coins and snow on our Christmas cards meant a program that showed Australian music, our music, made us feel bigger. Lenny Henry does a stand-up bit about the songs they will be singing around the piano at old people's homes in the future. I've got my money on The Angels' "Am I Ever Gonna See Your Face Again?"

Australian Idol

Once upon a time, long, long ago, when women smoked Alpine, men had moustaches and boning was something you did to chicken, not Jessica Rowe, we had *Young Talent Time*, *Countdown* and *New Faces*. Now we have *Australian Idol*. What these four shows have in common is that they are about discovering and promoting Australian musical talent. What makes *Australian Idol* different is that it's cynical, exploitative and it turns mediocrity into an extreme sport.

Although most contestants are not destined to become the next Kylie or Barnsey, this is way too much, way too soon. Sure, give the contestants their 15 minutes of fame. But not 17 weeks of intense scrutiny and exposure, 24 hours a day, seven days a week, only to have their fate determined by Sara, Lauren and Bree from year nine.

Let them sing into a hairbrush for a few more years, get their hearts broken and work in a drycleaners, so when their time comes they're hungry and they know who they are and what they want. These kids need time to develop their creative instincts – they don't need montages and stylists.

Most contestants will end up the under-ripe fruit that goes to market and doesn't get bought, just bruised. But Channel Ten is making too much money from the people phoning in to vote to care. So much money that it is impossible to find out how much.

I have a bit of a sweet spot for Dicko. And I miss him. Dicko was opinionated, straight-talking and at times off the mark, but he cared. His replacement, Kyle Sandilands, is a toxic shock-jock. Two weeks ago he got stuck into 17-year-old Jess's "jelly belly" after she had just given the performance of a lifetime. Shame on you, you tiny, tiny man.

Marcia Hines is so cool, she gets away with saying "you have an amazing gift, brother" and "it's wonderful to watch you grow into yourself, girl." And will someone tell Mark Holden that it is illegal to wear a V-neck jumper without anything underneath unless you are in *The Sopranos*? And that you should only talk about putting "fire in my wire and shiver in my quiver" if you are James Brown, or if you want your face punched in.

There is good crap and bad crap – and, as I always say, "all as a part of a balanced diet." But the Monday verdict show is industrial-strength, caterers-pack diabolical crap – 50 per cent recap and 50 per cent "One of these two will be leaving us tonight, who will it be? We'll find out after the break ..." That's not a show, that's an insult to the average viewer's intelligence. Please, God, let it be so.

Australian Idol is a simple game of musical chairs and I'm such a fan of voting people off that I believe it should extend to other programs, such as *Question Time*, *Neighbours* and *Mass for You at Home*. "To vote off Brendan the altar boy, SMS the word GENUFLECT to the number on your screen. After the break we have a peek at *Mass for You Up Late and Unconsecrated*."

Carols by Candlelight

'Twas the night before Christmas, and all through the house, not a creature was stirring, because mum was chucking her annual Christmas Eve spastic. "You lazy, useless, selfish kids. Oh no, don't get up. Don't get off your fat, ungrateful backsides and help your mother wrap the presents, peel the vegetables, vacuum the house, mop the floor, clean the windows, fold the clothes and set the table. You just sit there watching television while I slave my guts out so you can all have your fancy day tomorrow. Don't worry about your mother and her bad back, gammy leg, dodgy hip, splitting headache and [slightly louder] inoperable brain tumour the size of an eight-year-old child. I'll eat the burnt chop, sit on the broken chair in the draught. God forbid you think of anyone else but yourselves."

So there we'd sit, in front of the Rank Arena, paralysed with fear because not only was she wearing an apron but she was also wielding a knife. As we smelt the pork cooking and heard the Kenwood Mixmaster whipping up yet another pav, Karen Knowles sang "Silent Night." Well that's what we think she was singing. We had to lip-read, what with mum slamming things and swearing. Because what else would we be watching on Christmas Eve but *Carols by Candlelight*? Church? If you feel like it. But watching *Carols by Candlelight*? It's the law.

Where would we be without *Carols by Candlelight*? Probably somewhere in the Bagel Belt spinning a dreidel or in a café in Sydney Road sucking on a hookah.

The subject line of a recent email sent to me read: "Delta Goodrem headlines Vision Australia's *Carols by Candlelight*." The most over-rated performer in Australia will lead a "spectacular line-up of entertainers" in this year's concert, to be hosted by Ray Martin. Delta and Ray are joined by other people with nice hair and fake smiles, including Bert'n'Patti, Marina Prior, Anthony Callea and Dannii Minogue.

I find an evening full of old songs, fake breasts and small children holding candles while wearing highly flammable pyjamas deeply comforting. It's a couple of hours of harmless karaoke to get us in the mood for spending an entire day turning passive aggression into an extreme sport. But I can't bear the soap-stars' versions of the Christmas classics, complete with Mariah Carey vocal gymnastics, putting an entire scale where just a simple note will do. I like my carols like the Lord meant them to be: drawn-out, turgid and flat as a tack.

Every year one of the "artists" says, "I wish you could see what I see" and they cut to the swaying crowd holding their candles, reminding us of the importance of family, love and giving. When I was young I would think, "I wish you could see what I see. Mum has just thrown a pav at the television and now Brian Naylor looks like Father Christmas. And now she's screaming at us to put the washing in the car boot because Nana and Pop are coming over tomorrow."

Dancing with the Stars

My pants would be totally on fire if I said that I had ever watched even one episode of *Dancing with the Stars*. But I have gone to extreme lengths to sit in the audience of *Dancing* simply so you can be patchily enough informed to hang it on the show without even lifting a remote. Yes, it seems that I am too good to be true.

The audience letter tells me to "dress in after-five wear" (insert joke about pyjamas and Ugg boots here). It says: "We encourage you to stand out in the crowd by wearing colourful clothing. However, please do not wear any of the following: stripes, polka-dots or checks (so the gingham number is out because of the serious threat of strobing – whatever that is); solid white or black tops (you don't want dismembered heads in the audience); large logos on clothing (no product placement, fair enough); or open-toed shoes."

Open-toed shoes? Why? Terrorism? Safety? Clash with Naomi Robson? Then it hit me. Oh my God! Audience participation. Out comes the gold lamé, or the bridesmaid frock, and "three, and kick, and turn, and back, and four, five, six, seven, eight, and smile, two, three, four." I'm going to be a star!

So I line up with the unwashed masses outside the Seven studio and overhear conversations such as: "That so looks like Stacey's dog"; "You're only 30? That's because your Asian"; and "Tayla needs an en suite, she's just turned eight."

After the audience had been loaded, it was on with the show. The set looks great, the music is tight and the whole operation is run with extreme precision.

Daryl Somers walks down the stairs, maracas in hand, fake smile on his face and I think, "Please, Lord, don't let him sing." Daryl is jumpy, has no warmth and, unlike Bert, Rove, Ray or Adam Hills, doesn't look as if he is enjoying it at all. I doubt he's doing it for the money, more just the chance to get out of the house. The show may be live but the host's eyes are dead. Co-host Sonia Kruger is loving it, but we couldn't have her as a host because she's a chick.

It was samba night so, you guessed it, Harry High-pants central. The celebrity dancers are great value. The worse they were, the more we liked them.

Andrew Gaze was the audience's favourite, having a ball but more uncoordinated than Stephen Hawking. Tamsyn Lewis was so fake-tanned that she looked half-woman, half-Donatella Versace. Amanda Keller was a real trouper despite being described by judge Todd McKenney as "a soccer mum in sequins." And King Kouta? Good body, bad tips and trying so hard he was dancing with his tongue hanging out. Almost all for charity, which is to be commended.

It's good entertainment, it's good television, but it's not my cup of tea. But I could see how you could get hooked. Next series I'd like to see Bindi Irwin, Chopper Read, Amanda Vanstone and Eddie McGuire. I'm still practising, just in case – and two, and three, and turn, and kick, and two, three, four.

Where Are They Now

There are times when I can't help thinking, "If only television used its powers for good, not evil." These moments generally occur while I am tied to a chair with my eyelids taped open and forced at gunpoint to watch Channel Seven's *Where Are They Now.*

Fans of the show will be thrilled to know that *Where Are They Now* is back. But I doubt that fans will find that out from this column, because I'm fairly confident that no one who watches the show can read. Or has hands, because if they did, they'd flick over to another channel. Come to think of it, they mustn't have legs either, because they'd obviously turn the television off with their toes if they did. I've just realised that they probably don't have heads, because if these tragic armless, legless souls who can't read did, they would hurl themselves at the screen head-first.

Hosted by Melissa Doyle (a woman so disturbingly bubbly I want to pinch her 'til she cries) and David Koch (if it walks like a duck and quacks like a duck, it's probably an accountant), this cynical clip-show is what's known in the business as cheap and cheerful television. But at my place, it's what's known as that show mum makes us watch when we've been naughty.

The teaser at the start of each show seduces us with faces of up-and-coming blasts from the past. Each face elicits an immediate response: "Probably in jail," "Hopefully dead" and most frequently, "Who?"

If you want to know what happened to Rick Springfield (washed up loser), Jaleel White (me neither), Liesl from *The Sound Of Music* (flat-out doing "Where are they now?" shows) and Nikki Webster (the same as yesterday), tune in on Sunday night at 6.30. But keep in mind that you can never get that hour of your life back.

Like a school reunion, the idea of finding out what happened to these remember-whens is superficially fascinating for about ten seconds. To pad it out to an hour is just excruciating. When they start asking, "Ever wondered what happened to the voice of Dexter from *Perfect Match*?" you can smell the producers' desperation.

What the producers are saying to people asked to appear on these shows is basically "Hello, Greg Evans. Your career is over and people think you are dead. Feel like coming in and we will treat you like a celebrity for a few hours, then you can crawl back to your pathetic life? We will give you a cab voucher."

I'm no punctuation Nazi. Until recently I thought a semicolon was used to connect two sentences and a colon was involved in incidents like this: "I was standing on a chair changing the light globe, naked, fell down, and that's how I ended up with the tomato sauce bottle up there, doctor." I recently got the two mixed up in a rather unfortunate vacuum-cleaner-attachment-related grammatical faux pas. But what we should be asking is why is there is no question mark at the end of the title?

Where Are They Now is not all bad. They do have ad breaks.

Big Brother

Remember that Dutch reality show featuring a dying woman who was going to donate her kidney to one of three contestants? The outrage it generated was hilarious, considering *Big*

Brother is still on the box and thriving. At least *Queer Eye for the Straight Kidney*, *My Kidney Rules*, *Dancing with the Kidney*, *Kidneys Say the Darndest Things* or whatever it was called admitted being a case of "got you there, sucked in bad, suffer in your jocks." As opposed to *Big Brother*, which pounces around pretending to be a valuable social experiment providing quality entertainment to a discerning public.

Just in case you are a little confused, you were right the first time; it is boring, stupid and pointless. If I want to see self-obsessed bogan root-rats I'll just visit my cousin Kaiden and his wife Bree (don't worry, they can't read).

If you are a member of the Exclusive Brethren who has recently chewed through your restraints and joined the modern world, let me fill you in. *Big Brother* is what's called a reality show. Now, whenever you see the term "reality show" you should simply substitute the word "reality" with the word "shit" to get a more accurate idea of the genre.

A dozen of Australia's most annoying morons are forced to live in a compound with no outside contact or mod cons, under constant surveillance. Yes, a bit like being in the Brethren, just without the scarves. Maybe it should be called *Big Brethren*. The housemates get voted out one by one by the moron viewers until there is only one left. Who we will call Big Moron. Big Moron wins a crap car, money and free watered-down drinks at nightclub openings for the rest of his or her life. And if they are really lucky they will appear as a contestant on *Australia's Brainiest Big Brother Housemate*.

This is *Big Brother* 7. Once I could understand. But seven times? What did we do to deserve this? Simple. We kept on tuning in. Well, not we, I mean the people who read the *Herald Sun*. How far is this going to go? In 40 years will we end up with *Big Brother* 47 starring the grandchildren of the original housemates? I'll put money on it.

Big Brothel is simply a bunch of vapid media-whores in a televised chicken-pecking experiment. The housemates are shallow and the show is mind-numbing. My tip? For more fun buy binoculars and watch your own neighbours. It certainly amuses me no end.

SMS 199 TO SAVE, SMS 199 TO EVICT, where is the 199 number I can SMS TO DETONATE?

I should be more annoyed about this show but I'm just depressed. Good-looking young people should be out having loads of sex and drinking West Coast Coolers, not anesthetising themselves with this steaming pile of televisual excrement. And as for grown-ups, if watching this show is better than experiencing your own life, I'd suggest that you start looking at making some changes. May I suggest considering joining the Brethren.

Wife Swap

How much do I love *Wife Swap*? And when I say wife swap I'm talking the television show. Not wife-swapping as in the hotbed of adultery that is our kid's school's music trivia night. And by the way, grade-two Joshua's dad, stop pressing yourself up against me at parent–teacher nights or I will stab you in the scrotum with a large metal fork.

Did you hear that? That's the sound of the prep enrolments at our school skyrocketing by 4000.

OK, that stuff about the school is a load of toss. Back to *Wife Swap*. Yes, I know, it's reality TV. And yes, it is crap and not enlightening or nourishing on any level in any way, shape or form. And yes, it would be of more value to spend the money spent making this program on heroin for babies. But I find the show almost as fascinating and addictive as going through my neighbour's rubbish. This show is can't-turn-off TV. It's an anthropological study crossed with a sociological experiment crossed with a car accident. Involving circus freaks, extremists and ignorant morons. And a film crew.

Wife Swap USA is not to be confused with the original English version. The American version not only has dramatic opening credits complete with apocalyptic voice-over, but it sources the most polarised, deluded and narrow-minded families possible. If you enjoy judging people you will love *Wife Swap USA*.

A sun-worshipping, raw-food-eating, vegan animal-rights activist finds herself spending two weeks with a family of huntin', shootin', spankin' hicks from Goat Mountain. An eccentric artist who doesn't brush her hair or own a television swaps with a woman who devotes her entire life to her daughter's JonBenet-style beauty pageants.

The most compelling episode so far this season was the one in which a gay male psychologist (father of two teenage girls) became the "wife" of a gun totin' trailer-trash unemployed sadistic loser from the Bible belt. This homophobic creep would not let his "wife" sleep under his roof and his pastor advised the creep to do the Christian thing and treat his visitor like vermin because of his sexuality. Yet he had no moral issue with beating his three young boys with what looked like a cricket bat. This week an etiquette expert who forces her children to dress in formal attire for five-course dinners eaten off fine china swaps with a woman who encourages her children to have food fights and burping competitions at restaurants. You can't help being repelled by both.

Every episode ends with the feeling "I'm a freak. You're a freak and that's OK" and each family seems to take away something. Including the Bible-bashing freak, who said, "It took a queen to make my wife a queen."

I enjoy *Wife Swap* because after the show I take a moment to reflect on my own life, think about the choices that I have made. I always feel … how can I put this without sounding superior and smug? Well, I feel superior and smug.

Super Nanny

There are many ways for people to feel good about themselves. Some go to the gym, some meditate, while others help people less fortunate than themselves. When I want to feel good about myself I watch *Super Nanny.*

I was so excited I couldn't sleep last Thursday night because the next day was Bloody Grouse Friday, return of the hit series *Super Nanny.* Does television get any better than watching saucy straight-talking English nanny Jo Frost go into the homes of barking-mad families to expose children so hideous that it makes you understand why some mothers eat their young? I think not.

The first time we watched *Super Nanny* my partner and I were stunned; he by the behaviour of the children and me at how clean the family's house was. I remember the smugness in his voice when he turned to me and said, "Our children would never do anything like that," to which I replied, "Well certainly not on television." Our three boys relished watching kids behaving badly as much as we enjoyed judging lazy fathers and indulgent mothers.

Super Nanny is not just must-see TV, it's addictive. Who could forget the Jeans family from the first season? The parents waited 16 years into their marriage before having Andra followed 18 months later by twins Jessie and Leah. Three blonde-haired little girls. Each child individual in their own way, but all three deeply evil and the spawn of Satan.

Remember the Burnetts, parents of two sets of twins aged three and 16 months and one older child at school? That's right, five kids under six. The parents both work full time, the father from home and the mother as a schoolteacher. The children were in no child care *at all* and the parents had no help *whatsoever* yet they couldn't work out why they weren't managing. Here's a tip, because you are *greedy*.

Why don't these parents know about boundaries and consequences? Why are they so afraid to discipline their kids? Do they think that if they say, "No, Braden/Clareen/Jonisha, you cannot kick, punch and spit at your nana, it's her birthday," that the kids will turn around and stab them in their sleep?

The fact that these people let a camera team into their home shows how desperate these parents are for answers, or at the very least apprehended violence orders against their children. The genius who came up with this idea should be given some kind of award for restoring the confidence of so many parents who feel that they are not up to scratch. And I'm not talking about the freaks who let Nanny Jojo into their homes, I'm talking about the viewers at home.

You could be excused for thinking that this program is nothing more than a freak show masquerading as infotainment, but anecdotal evidence suggests that it has been an enormous help to many families controlling their terrorists (no offence to any suicide bombers or religious fundamentalists that may be reading this).

What I find hard to understand is why people need her to come into their homes when Nanny Jojo does the same thing, every time. At the first sight of "unasseptable" behaviour she gets down to the troll's level, reads them the riot act and it's the naughty step/chair/mat/point/pants for one minute per year of age. It is heartening, encouraging and a little disappointing to see the evil little freaks respond to her techniques. There goes our kids being a good house in a bad street.

I find the difference between the US and UK families astonishing. The US kids tend to be brats (tantrums, petulance, passive aggression) while the UK kids are generally thugs (swearing, spitting, head-butting). The US moms tend to be thin, stressed-out and fairly affluent while UK mums are overweight, under-educated and struggling financially. It's comforting to see bad parenting is not class-specific. You can find morons in any demographic.

And what do we think about these kids and their revolting behaviour being exposed on television without the child's consent? Is this a new form of child abuse? Are the inevitable lawsuits simply a matter of time?

A program on teaching us how to parent was a logical step. Television has already educated us on how to cook, garden, travel, solve crime and, in the case of *Big Brother*, act like dickheads. *Super Nanny* has been so successful I must admit that I am surprised that we haven't seen *Queer Eye for the Straight Child, My Ritalin Rules* or a show about four-year-old girls simply called *The Mole.*

Dr Phil

I don't watch daytime television. Maybe it's because watching daytime TV feels a bit like having cigarettes, ice-cream and Burger Rings for breakfast. Or it could be because watching daytime TV does kill you.

I must admit that I do appear on daytime telly occasionally. Only pensioners, breastfeeding mothers and gym junkies have ever seen me. And, according to one of the show's producers, prisoners are big watchers. On hearing this, Dicko – who had just appeared on the same show – said something along the lines of, "How about that then? Right now some jail bait with a pretty mouth is popping one with your name on it." Should I take it as a compliment? Or should I appear wearing a burqa from now on?

Sitting in make-up, I have watched the show that I am about to appear on and, although I have hung it on the Inflatable Magic Recliner, the Ab King Pro and the Gale Force Cyclonic Vacuum, I have been tempted to purchase the hand-held sewing machine.

My sister mentioned Dr Phil to me the other day. I said "Who?" She said, "Dr Phil. You know, psychologist, tells people to get their shit together, used to be on Oprah." When I told her that I didn't watch daytime TV she pretty much called me a liar ending with, "Yeah, right. I've seen your house and you obviously don't spend your day cleaning."

She was not the last to mention Dr Phil. People who dabble in daytime telly, in the same way that some people who use drugs consider themselves users as opposed to junkies, have also held my hands, looked me in the eye and said, "You've got to watch Dr Phil."

With episode titles such as "Spouses Who Let Themselves Go," "People Pleasers and Doormats" and "the Dark Side of Cheerleading," I was expecting some Jerry Springer "My Dog Married My Guinea Pig's Lesbian Lover" action. Or a bit of Rikki Lake "I Turned Tricks in My Son's School Car Park to Pay for a Makeover." But no. Dr Phil tells losers, thugs, whingers and drama queens to get over it, grow up and change.

In the same way that some people only read *Penthouse* for the articles, some people only watch daytime television for Dr Phil. Sure, I am alarmed by the number of people with names such as Duane and Amber on the show, the fact that a psychologist gets a standing ovation before ripping into people in front an audience of millions. And, for the millionth time, I wonder why people subject themselves to this kind of humiliation. He's also proud of everyone and I hate that word. It's patronising, condescending and implies a paternalistic sense of ownership. And let's not mention his disregard for the basic principles of psychology.

Don't you hate it when you have picked up some pop psychology bestseller and find yourself nodding as things hit a chord? That's what it's like watching Dr Phil. He talks sense and he gives viewers helpful strategies. Let's face it: if they are watching daytime television, chances are they need as much help as they can get.

Cheaters

It is time for me to introduce you to the hidden jewel in Seven's crown, *Cheaters*. Don't thank me. By the time you get to the end of this column you'll wish that you'd never been born. After watching this show I burnt my clothes, had my couch exorcised and shaved off all my hair.

What finally compelled me to hold my nose, suspend my disbelief and voluntarily inflict this US reality show on myself was duty to my readers. And this email from my mate Sub: "Have you seen *Cheaters*? It's a beauty! On tonight's ep, girl forgives cheatin', Christian, dope-smoking, drinkin', lyin' fiancé … because God asked her to."

If you find yourself thinking, "There must be more to this show than red-necked root-rats," you'd be wrong. I have infected myself with this horrific strain of the *Cheaters* virus in the hope that this column may give you all immunity. It may save you all the humiliation of seeing your own reflection in the TV screen and coming to the tragic realisation that you are watching this televisual slag-heap. At least I got paid for it.

The show's opening attempts to dispel any suspicion that this may be exploitation repackaged as low-cost television by explaining that "*Cheaters* presents to you inspirational chronicles of humankind." There is talk of "the heroic men and women who overcome the challenges of relationships and restore health and happiness to their lives by taking charge and holding accountable the unfaithful."

Rigid and emotionless host Tommy Grand opens the show by introducing Ken, a 61-year-old gent who has requested that *Cheaters* "measures the true dimension of his fiancée's purported love" a month before their marriage.

Ken describes his partner as a "clean, decent, honest woman" who has raised his suspicions by doing things such as nicking out to visit a friend and not coming back for five days. As you do.

Ken gives the *Cheaters* crack team the nod and it's surveillance and secret cameras a plenty. Lo and behold, the fiancée is indeed banging the best man and this "lack of integrity" is documented and shown to a shaken Ken.

Ken and the *Cheaters* crew enter his home and the fiancée is caught on the job, with the best man, all to the tune of "What's Love Got To Do with It?"

The best man hotfoots it, and Ken explains to his remorseful fiancée that he called *Cheaters* because he believed it was the most Christian thing to do. All the while, the couple watches the footage of the fiancée and best man doing the pink thing. Milk that human misery! Zoom in on that degradation! Tight shot of that shame!

The Australian *Cheaters* website has a section "The top 15 ways to tell if your partner is cheating." No. 12 is, "Check your spouse's underwear, look for sexual secretions. We can provide a test, which detects minute traces of ejaculation. Works on both men and women."

But if you are after a *Cheaters* thong and matching mug for mum for Mother's Day, you'll have to pop over to the American website.

Pucker Up

Very few things impress me. Wealth? Boring. Beauty? Predictable. Name-dropping? Don't bother, I've written for Frankie J. Holden, the Village People and Anna-Nicole Smith, so let me assure you that I've had my 15 minutes on the celebrity sun-lounge. But if you are talking bizarre medical conditions or impressive party tricks I am mouth agape, camera out, gagging for a snap. Which is why I am going to give *Pucker Up: The Fine Art of Whistling* a damn fine plug.

I knew a man who played the spoons like a god and a girl who could burp the entire alphabet in one hit. I'm no slouch either when it comes to physical prowess. What's my party trick, apart from turning up to a dinner party, skolling a bottle of red on an empty stomach and calling everyone a bunch of wankers just before passing out halfway through the second verse of "Knees Up Mother Brown"? My party trick is that I can fit my entire fist in my mouth. No, no, please sit down; I'm just a very ordinary person.

We're all impressed by physical prowess, including my four-year-old, who saw me clicking my fingers the other day and said, "Can I have a go?" He's not the sharpest knife in the drawer. He's an idiot savant, just without the savant bit.

Pucker Up is a documentary about the International Whistling Convention held, of course, in the capital of whistling, Louisburg USA; a town complete with whistling school and museum. Each year the convention crowns the International Grand Champion Whistler. And man, can these mother-puckers whistle. They could whistle a fish finger through a cat.

The first bloke we meet whistles so well that he communicates with birds – the bird whisperer if you will. And what does he do for a living? He kills chickens. Then we meet a professional whistler who has the personalised numberplate WHISTLR. He dreams of being invited to whistle with great orchestras. Next up, a man who has suffered several divorces, countless tragic deaths and lost everything to hurricanes three times. He claims that when you whistle you forget everything. And then we have the European bloke who whistles like a bird and smokes like a chimney.

There is great reminiscing about the golden age of whistling when whistlers were given the respect they deserve, and mentions of the whistling greats like Fred Lowery, the blind Elvis Presley of whistling. One whistler bemoans that when the odd whistler turns up on Letterman they're treated as a stupid human trick.

I love a good doco and you know what? *Pucker Up* has it all. The extreme version of something we have a basic understanding of, a couple of bizarre historical facts, some scientific explanation and a few people's journeys ending in a showdown so hilarious I lost 5 kilos from laughing. But it's the man who says that he got over the death of his daughter by whistling that makes you believe in the healing power of this simple and almost extinct pleasure.

Peking to Paris

Twelve years, 15 kilos, three kids and at least four hairstyles ago I took the slow boat to China and did the Trans-Siberian Express. I had been living in Tokyo for 15 months working as a ~~prostitute~~ English teacher and I was bang-up to slum it. Nepal was too obvious so it was off to Beijing with $800 cash, a denim jacket and a totally manufactured veneer of cool in order to convince people that I was worldly and enigmatic. Which worked quite effectively; that is, until I drank my body weight in a Chinese beer that used formaldehyde as preservative and threw up in my own hair. On the first night.

What I was gagging for by doing this trip was a riveting travel story of near death, true love or kidnap, but unfortunately everything went to plan. The train rattled through

China (nice place to visit but you wouldn't want to do Falun Gong there), Mongolia, where we lived on mutton and Passiona for days, and finally Russia, the only place in the world, apart from Reservoir, where people get married wearing tracksuits.* All without so much as a sign offering YOUR NAME ON A GRAIN OF RICE.

Which is probably why I am enjoying *Peking to Paris* so much. This four-part series retraces an expedition driving from Peking to Paris in 100-year-old cars. The 1907 odyssey proved once and for all that the age of the motorcar had truly arrived. To put it in perspective, at the time this journey was today's equivalent of flying to the moon on a Tamagotchi.

Think about it: no roof, no doors, no windscreen, no mobile phones, no roads, no seatbelts and no airbags. That wasn't an adventure, it was a body bag waiting to happen.

People with a limited imagination and a low intellect consider endurance television, be it *Survivor*, *The Amazing Race* or an interview with Naomi Robson, a cheap laugh. They are morons who find watching insane people with fire in their belly and low self-esteem make idiots of themselves incredibly funny. And I am one of them.

Peking to Paris is a fun ride that is part endurance, part travel and part history. It's a little repetitive and predictable with meltdowns, breakdowns and backdowns, but that is the nature of the beast. China was frustrating, Mongolia was barren and Russia was full of piss-heads. No surprises there.

The group of predominantly Australian petrol-heads driving these old jalopies range from an uptight brain surgeon to a "she'll be right, fair suck of the sav, pass me a tinnie will ya mate" mechanic. The thread that really makes this fairly unremarkable show watchable is the engaging voice-over from cartoonist and industrial-strength optimist Warren Brown. His enthusiasm is infectious to the point of terminal at times.

I've seen the end and I can assure you that it is worth the wait. Although I'm certain that it was a life-changing experience, next time I reckon they will take the plane.

---

* I grew up in Reservoir, so get off your high horse.

The Winner's Guide to the Nobel Prize

When I think of Sweden I think Volvos, ABBA, Ikea and Princess Mary of Denmark.

Sweden, Denmark. Same thing. They eat rollmops, sit in saunas hitting each other with sticks and speak English better than we do. And they're better-looking than we are. I better stop there.

In 2005 two Australians, Robin Warren and Barry Marshall, were awarded the Nobel Prize for discovering that stomach ulcers were caused by a bacterium and not stress. *The Winners' Guide to the Nobel Prize* follows these two Australian scientists through Sweden's biggest week of the year, Nobel Prize week, and retraces their 20-year journey from the initial discovery, to shaking hands with the King of Sweden.

The pair see themselves as Felix and Oscar from *The Odd Couple*. I see them more as Mick and Keith from the Rolling Stones with slightly more access to (prescription) drugs. Pathologist Robin Warren describes himself as an "introverted, hard-to-get-on-with, grumpy old man." His daughter-in-law says he is "a monomaniac" and that he "can be a bit difficult." I love the moment when this scientific genius is off to receive the Nobel Prize but can't work out the seatbelt in the taxi to the airport.

His partner, professor of medicine Barry Marshall, has matinee looks, a charismatic presence and is a grandfather of three. When you see the old photos, Barry seemed to be under the impression that every month in the '70s was Movember. Colleagues described young Barry as "a pretentious whipper-snapper." Barry happily put his stomach lining where his mouth was and gave himself an ulcer by skolling the *Helicobacter Pylori* bacteria. He loves a bit of sizzle, our Barry.

It is glorious to see these two daggy, dedicated scientists being treated like rock stars during their week in Sweden. They got, not just 15 minutes of fame, but a whole week on the celebrity sun lounge. No drugs, hookers or paparazzi but plenty of autograph signings and chauffeured cars.

I, like every other untalented, unremarkable person who can't sing, act or catch a ball, loathe the way Australia venerates its sporting "heroes" and "artists" over the stunning achievements of our less sexy (but more profound) professions. This show is a wonderful example of how science is treated on the ABC.

The ABC has nurtured talent such as Karl Kruszelnicki, Clio Cresswell, Adam Spencer and Cindy Pan. I loved Karina Kelly, former host of the science program *Catalyst* because she was also the narrator of *Bananas in Pyjamas*. That's the ABC for you, everybody pitches in when there is work to be done.

I teared up when Barry and Robin received their award. They fought and won a heroic battle. Barry's advice to young scientists is, "Work hard, try to keep balance in your life and just in case, always be nice to Swedish people." Danish. Whatever.

You can have Barnesy and Farnsey, B1 and B2 and the Woodies. Barry and Robin get my vote for greatest Australian duo.

The God Delusion

Richard Dawkins is a scientist and passionate atheist who has produced a stunning, thoroughly researched and expertly executed work that flatly denies the existence of God and illustrates what a destructive force religion is. Even in its mildest form. This provocative and entertaining ride will have some believers coming out the other end as atheists. And every Bible basher, Torah toter and Koran carrier calling the ABC to complain.

As I watched this masterpiece unfold, I couldn't remember the last time I had seen something so brilliant on the idiot box. Dawkins unapologetically refuses to treat religion differently from any other subject. There is no tiptoeing in fear of "offending" anyone (how you can offend people with truth is beyond me).

Dawkins has harnessed his skill as a scientist, his hunger for truth and his rage to prove that God is a delusion that's infecting the world. He refers to "the process of non-thinking called faith" and bemoans "that the idea of a divine creator belittles the elegant reality of the universe." He liberates the viewer with the conclusion that "atheism is life-affirming in a way religion can never be."

Atheists will watch this show and feel as if they have died

and gone to heaven as they see a bloke far more smarterer than themselves poke that animal in the cage. The fundamentalists, the evangelicals, the dabblers and the moderates all cop it. Dawkins dismembers the lot with a scalpel. It's intoxicating for born-again atheists like myself. I have taken the Flying Spaghetti Monster as my Lord and personal saviour. That's right. I am a Pastafarian.

Atheism is, it seems, the new black. Dawkins' offering will not simply be preaching to the converted but actually convert fence-sitters with truth and reason. He describes the God of the Old Testament as "the most unpleasant character in all fiction. Jealous and proud of it. Petty, vindictive, unforgiving and racist. An ethnic cleanser urging his people on to acts of genocide."

Then Moses cops it. Dawkins quotes a Bible story and asks: "How is this story morally distinguishable from Hitler's rape of Poland or Saddam Hussein's massacre of the Kurds or the Marsh Arabs?"

Dawkins' masterful command of the language and his glorious Britishness are a delight throughout: "So Jesus had himself tortured and executed for a symbolic sin by a non-existent individual. Nobody not brought up in the faith could reach to any verdict other than barking mad." He tells us that "killing for God is not just hideous murder but utterly ridiculous."

On Sunday night, if you listen carefully, you'll hear atheists all over Australia leaning back in their chairs, putting their feet on the coffee table and saying, "I'm with him." And I'll be one of them.

Choir of Hard Knocks

There are millions of reasons to switch off the telly. *Choir of Hard Knocks* is one of the few reasons to turn it on. One of the best shows from last year was SBS' *Nerds FC*, which followed a bunch of nerds who were transformed into a soccer team. The ABC's *Choir of Hard Knocks* turns a bunch of homeless and disadvantaged people into a choir. I cheered when I watched *Nerds FC*. I cried like a baby watching *Choir of Hard Knocks*.

Choir director Jonathon Welch is a renowned tenor, a brilliant singing teacher and a beautiful, beautiful man. Recently returning to Melbourne after living abroad for many years, Welch was compelled to form the choir after reading an article about a choir for homeless people in Montreal.

There were no auditions and no selection process. The word was sent out through flyers, community groups and word of mouth. If you were up for it, there was a chair for you and a cuppa at the end. The choir currently has about 50 regulars.

This is no *Young Talent Time*. People who suffer mental illnesses, sleep rough and have problems with demons, have meltdowns, spin-outs and, in one case, issues with personal hygiene. That's what makes this show so heart-warming, and so heartbreaking. You can hear their rocky journey through their voices, which makes their happiness punch you in the guts and makes your heart sing.

Choir of Hard Knocks is not a reality show. It's a documentary series. And it gave me goosebumps. Welch gathered together a bunch of folk who've done it tough and with his passion for music and his desire to share his talent and experience has given the choir members joy, hope and purpose. To listen to people who have battled, and will continue to battle, sing "I Can See Clearly Now," "Love is in the Air" and Leonard Cohen's "Hallelujah" was spine-tingling. But what had me howling was listening to them sing Cold Chisel's "Flame Trees." On stage. With Jimmy Barnes.

Choir of Hard Knocks is a five-parter. Don't worry if you've missed the first two. This week the choir has a session in a recording studio funded by their busking revenue. Watching the singers' faces as they listen to their own CD was magical. Welch was overcome with emotion as he told them, with tears running down his face, "That's you singing. And they're your voices." The decency and dignity the singers find through the simple but profound act of lifting their voices together is exhilarating. Singing for the sheer joy, for the catharsis, for the sense of belonging and the feeling of achievement.

The Choir of Hard Knocks has no funding. They operate purely on the revenue collected from the sales of their CDs and their concert tickets. There's a CD to accompany the series and a concert at Melbourne Town Hall in July. Support these dedicated people who remind us that the journey is the destination. And sing along if you know the words.

9/11: Falling Man

Too many of the hours spent sitting in front of the box you come away from remembering nothing and feeling empty. You look shamefully at all those CDs you own and books you've painstaking moved several times and know that you should have spent your time more valuably. Instead you stare blankly at a screen. Actually, I don't mean you. I mean me.

The media is at its finest and most honourable when it is scrutinising itself. Think *Media Watch*, *Frontline* and *The Chaser's War on Everything*. Which is why I reckon that if you watch anything this week you must check out *9/11: Falling Man*, another stunning and masterful documentary produced for BBC's Channel 4.

It is made with a light hand and an inquiring mind. This compelling piece of television follows journalist Tom Junod's journey to identify the man in the famous photo of a person falling to his death from the World Trade Center on September 11, 2001, captured by photographer Richard Drew. Junod came across people who, for religious reasons, refused even to consider that it may have been their loved one (people who commit suicide don't go to heaven, apparently). Coroners refused to admit that there were any jumpers, only people who fell. The suggestion being that jumping was gutless and some sort of cop-out. There was also a man hoping to find an image of his wife jumping as he searched for peace despite crushing grief.

I remember at the time reading reports of people jumping and wondering why I saw no images of them. I was not as glued to the whole circus as most people because I gave birth on 9 September, so I put it down to the few newspapers I was reading. In truth the images were published quite widely on 12 September but were rarely seen again.

Why? Drew's image was branded distasteful, exploitative and voyeuristic. I would call *Big Brother* distasteful, exploitative and voyeuristic but it has been with us since 2001.

The official images now stand, plane ploughs into building. Another plane ploughs into building. People caked in dust and blood running from the scene. Buildings collapse. Heroic rescuers. Cut to Osama bin Laden in cave.

I believe that omitting the images of the gore, mutilation and carnage is deception in itself. Bring out your dead. I am up for it. I'm an adult. How dare you dilute the truth. Don't protect me. Just run this line first: WARNING. THE FOLLOWING MAY CONTAIN THE TRUTH.

European magazines are renowned for showing much gorier images than we see and those countries are, in general, far more reluctant to go into war. When the late Graham Perkin, former editor of the *Age*, had people trying to persuade him against publishing a rather confronting photograph during the Vietnam War, apparently he said something along the lines of, "Let 'em choke on their Weeties." I'd like to see more of that, thanks.

Beaconsfield

The most memorable flash of the Beaconsfield mining disaster coverage for me was the moment I saw Eddie McGuire down at the Beaconsfield Pub holding a beer and saying "mate" a lot. Like many people, my first thought was, "Haven't these people been through enough?"

The only thing more transparent than Eddie pretending to be Beaconsfield's new best friend to persuade the miners to sell his network their story was Bill Shorten using these people's personal tragedy as leverage to increase his profile to become Labor leader.

Maybe I am a little too cynical. God forbid I confuse a

politician's magnanimous love for mankind as branding a tumultuous event with his smug face simply to propel his career forward. Mmmm, smell that parliamentary superannuation. And while we are on the subject of bandwagons, whoever came up with the idea of getting the Prime Minister addressing the nation by a mobile phone on loudspeaker through a microphone held by Tracy Grimshaw after the miners surfaced is a media genius.

The media coverage was so huge that, not only did Oprah call, but apparently Osama Bin Laden was watching and could totally relate to the miners, because he lives underground as well. The only problem is that now he wants an iPod. And icy poles. And he wants to know who the Foo Fighters are.

I was gripped by this extraordinary story of the rescuers' heroic efforts, the miners' amazing mental toughness and this community's enviable closeness. This three-act narrative with the bittersweet ending was media-friendly, emotive and, if you believe the commercial television stations, uniquely Australian. (But don't tell that to the families of the workers killed in Chinese mines every day.) If you believe what you see on the telly, the only way the miners' story could have been more Australian is if they had come out of the mine on Simpson's donkey.

Stories such as September 11, the Boxing Day tsunami and the death of Princess Diana give us as a nation and we as humans a rare opportunity to experience real emotions together, resulting in an illusion of community that we crave. That's why the media thrive on them.

All of Australia suddenly cared about the fortunes and misfortunes of a small mining town. These communities are really suffering and it's a disgrace that it takes a tragedy like this for us to take notice. For a week or two. The liquid loyalties of the media means that after all the hullabaloo they will pack up their caravans and wait patiently for the next disaster. I can't help wondering if struggling mining communities around the nation won't re-enact this scenario for the attention and the bucks.

It's wonderful that we all barracked for them, prayed for them and rejoiced together but I think the media's vulturedom and their brazen alignment with this display of courage is shameful.

But yes, I'll be watching. Our Todd and Our Brant, hosted by Our Tracy.

SBS and Sex

I enjoy watching SBS for the in-depth global analysis from a multicultural perspective, the stunning array of creativity and, like the rest of you, the hardcore pornography clumsily masquerading as "human interest" and "biological diversity." When I see that a show MAY CONTAIN COARSE LANGUAGE AND SURGICAL PROCEDURES sure, I'm interested. But if they are talking ADULT THEMES, NUDITY AND SIMULATED SEX, I am turning on the answering machine, pouring a glass of wine and vacillating between laughing like a lunatic and screaming as if I am being stabbed. Now the World Cup and Tour de France are over, the SBS 10 o'clock Friday-night sex spot is back. (And don't pretend that you've never heard of it. We're all fascinated by deviants, freaks and losers.)

Thanks to *Big Brother*, I now know what "turkey slapping" is. But thanks to SBS, I have been "informed" and "educated" by "documentaries" about people who prefer sex with amputees, a man who could get aroused only when wearing ten layers of rubber and a gasmask, and a piece made by a man with a trouser snake the size of a Tic Tac. In Tiny Todger Man's cry for help, *My Penis And I*, he talked to his mum about his old man's old fella, visited a cosmetic surgeon, attended a Small Penis Society meeting (don't ask) and had a plaster cast made of his willy. Laugh? I lost 5 kilos I laughed so much. Not about the size of his pink skin flute but that he felt compelled to make a documentary about it.

Here is a list of shows you may have missed (or recorded and labelled Australian Open Women's Final 1998): *Stacked Like Me*, *The Sperminator*, *Why Men Wear Frocks* and *My 100,000 Lovers*. All paid for by the government. That's why they call this place the Lucky Country. My mum saw a woman sticking spaghetti down her daks on the telly a while back with a rather serious voice-over. I can only assume that it was something from the 10 o'clock slot, unless she was watching *Today Tonight*. The motivation behind screening these kind of programs is almost as alarming as my mother asking if I had taped it.

An American kids-TV host was recently sacked by PBS for appearing in a satirical sex-education video seven years ago. Yet across the Atlantic, Britain's Channel Four is planning an entire "Wank Week" dedicated to the important issue of masturbation. Included will be documentary about a mass masturbation for charity with the working title wank-a-thon and a documentary about compulsive masturbators. The producers already have a 20-a-day man and are searching for another wanker. Note to self: Must call Eddie McGuire.

If you missed last night's *A Pornographic Affair*, don't despair. There's plenty more where that came from in the coming months with titles such as *Eros under the Swastika* (the Third Reich gets to third base), *Sexual Intelligence* (the Mensa club for perverts), and get your dancing shoes on and your pants off for everyone's nana's favourite: *Pornography: The Musical*. It's kind of like South Pacific, but in the nude.

The Einstein Factor

I have a thing for geeks, nerds and freaks. Not in an "aren't they cute" way. More in a "don't take a restraining order out on me. I really do love you. I am not a stalker," kind of a way.

The Einstein Factor is nerd-loving paradise. It is also the best quiz show on television bar none. No frills, no fancy gift shop, no fancy people, no fancy electricity. I reckon there was more money spent producing *It's Academic* than *The Einstein Factor*.

This show is solid old-fashioned entertainment. The contestants don't leave with a diamond-set moment from Bruce and Walsh. Or *The Einstein Factor* board game. You know what they get? Bugger all.

I'm fairly sure that they have to supply their own sandwiches and thermos as well. And it's BYOB: Bring Your Own Buzzer. The grand final winner gets a trophy made by the *Play School* art department. But what more could you desire than the glory of being crowned King or Queen of the Nerds and still be tucked up in bed with a Bonox and a good book by 9.30?

The Einstein Factor has people who know an alarming

amount about a subject so obscure that you can't help wondering if they are making up the topic or taking the piss. Byzantine Emperor Romanus I Lecapenus? Never heard of him. An expert on *Are You Being Served*? Come off it.

Despite being world experts, the show's contestants will never make a living out of their lifetime obsession. And how do I know? My special subject is the life and career of Olivia Newton-John between *Grease* and *Xanadu* and I can assure you that there is no money in that.

The contestants are a breath of fresh air with not a smarty-pants to be seen. They are the antitheses of wankers. They are what you would get if you put a *Big Brother* contestant into an opposite machine. Being on the show is their time to shine. And they do, in their endearing "I'd rather die than draw attention to myself, no it's fine I'll just stand, you take the chair" kind of way.

This little dark-horse of a show averages an audience of a million viewers. And so it should. It's bloody grouse. It's also programmed perfectly at 6.30 pm Sunday. One of the writers tells me that the ratings spike in the winter as people are watching the telly while they eat their soup. I can smell the slippers and cardies from here.

Peter Berner is funny, endearing and nerdy enough to pull it off and he looks as if he is having a ball. *Junior Einstein*, coming up in August, is worth tuning in to if only to see the young girl whose special subject is Hitler.

But the topics are the real stars; Australian Metropolitan Horse Racing of the 1960s, *The Young & The Restless*, The Life and Career of Evel Knievel, Vexillology. Some people reckon that the contestants should really get out more. But I love them, just the way they are. And I have footage of them in the shower to prove it.

Nerds FC

No longer is the SBS 10 o'clock perverted freaks sex-slot the highlight of my Friday night viewing. Now it's *Nerds FC*.

For those of you who have not seen the show, here's the deal. Experts coach 14 nerds for three months, all culminating in Nerds FC playing a soccer match against a professional team in front of 25,000 people. Participating in this show has not only given the nerds their first opportunity to see real-live humans since the 1998 *Star Trek* convention but also their first reason to bathe in 15 years.

Reality television has allowed us to sticky beak as celebrities become ballroom dancers, Christian fundamentalist virgins transform into rock stars and, in the case of *Big Brother*, attention-seeking dickheads emerge as even bigger attention-seeking dickheads. But *Nerds FC* has something that the other shows of this genre don't. And I am not talking about men with the ability to recite the dialogue from the *Star Wars* trilogy backward. This show has dignity. I know you are waiting for the joke but I can assure you that on *Nerds FC* not even the voice-over is taking the piss.

I am in love with these nerds and I adore this show. These guys are generous, beautiful souls. If you are after bitching, back-stabbing or voting off you won't get it here. It's a breath of fresh air to see know-alls, not wankers, on the telly doing something to get fit – not famous.

So far, with three episodes to go here are my top five moments.

1. As the team walks towards the trainers for the first time one coach turned to the other and said, "The closer they get the worse they look."

2. One nerd suggested they call themselves Team 3.141592653589.

3. Watching their faces when they find out that their first match is against women.

4. Watching their faces when they find out that their second match is against prisoners.

5. When they wanted to elect Tim as captain simply because his surname was Kirk so they could be led by Captain Kirk.

Watching these men with the IQ of Stephen Hawking and the gross motor co-ordination to match attempting to dance the samba was also a high point.

But I am warning you, these guys are hardcore, soft-bellied, industrial strength nerds, unlike the ersatz nerds on *The Einstein Factor*. These nerds are not only aware that they have no life but can prove it mathematically. When these guys try to turn a woman on they look for the switch.

Nerds FC's Nick says on their website: "I consider myself a nerd because I focus my not-inconsiderable powers on the acquisition and comprehension of knowledge at the expense of all other aspects of my life." My first thought was, "Feel free to get a life at any stage." My second thought was, "It seems he already has one."

Tune in. If you don't, I will send the nerds around and they will defrag your computer, prove that they are not on a first-name basis with personal hygiene and then entertain you by listing every prime number up to 27 digits.

Play School

WARNING: the following may contain naked dolls, well-respected actors waddling like ducks and cars made of toilet rolls and pipe-cleaners.

Play School turns 40 on 18 July and it doesn't look a day over ten. Sure, Jemima's let herself go, Big Ted's had some work done and Humpty, well, not only has he been feeding in the good paddock but that hair looks as real as Michael Jackson's nose. But with 1781 episodes under its belt and more than a million viewers a week it's still going off like a frog in a sock.

The calm, happy voices and tinkling piano music lulling preschoolers into a trance of contentment is for parents the equivalent to a handful of Valium and half a bottle of scotch. When your children watch *Play School* you feel as if you are giving them a salad sandwich on bread made by organic lesbian nuns and a wheatgrass juice hand-pressed by the Dalai Lama.

Grown-ups love *Play School* too. I have two preschoolers and when childless people sitting at our bench drinking long blacks, passionately discussing the post-structuralist impact of Pre-Raphaelite Pro Hart, hear that familiar tune – "There's a bear in there/ And a chair as well/ There are people with games ..." – you should see their faces. They squeal *Play School*!! and run like girls to the television and marvel that it hasn't changed a bit. They then proceed to bore me with dull stories of their favourite presenters until I stab them in the face with a fork.

You can tell a lot about people by which *Play School* window they wanted picked.

SQUARE: Conservative, fond of routine, partial to pain.

CIRCLE: Dreamers, idealists, bed-wetters.

ARCH: Creative, experimental, often not on a first-name basis with personal hygiene.

TRIED TO WORK OUT THE ORDER: Controlling, manipulative, tendency to genocide.

Play School is not immune to controversy. Who could forget the furore over the kid with two mummies? Or Benita at the Logies a few years ago wearing a top that made many of the fans say, "I can see her boobies." Or the disappearance of the original Little Ted, last seen in 1973 in the possession of a stagehand heading off to Honkers.

I quite liked Mr Squiggle but I must admit that I was a little freaked out by the rocket. "Yes, Miss Jane. Turn it around, Miss Jane. And again, Miss Jane. Mmm, I love your sheer stockings and your stilettos, Miss Jane." I watched Humphrey growing up as well, and sure, I loved the big brown bear with no pants. *Sesame Street* was OK too but it just didn't feel like home. Not like *Play School*. The presenters acted in the calm and uncondescending way that we wished our own parents would. But they were too busy making shepherd's pie, getting stuck into the cooking sherry or folding up Project Compassion boxes.

Happy birthday, *Play School*.

English Comedy

Right now if the Poms started bombing nursing homes, running over kittens with lawnmowers or eating roasted babies I'd forgive them because of the wild orgy of English comedy I indulged in last night. I gorged on the new series of *Extras* and the last season of *Little Britain* and I was in comedy heaven. It was more fun than being turkey slapped by Daryl Somers. Don't ask me how I know.

My partner said to me that my last few columns have been unnecessarily cruel and vicious in slagging off appalling shows. I was so deeply touched by such praise that I almost took his chains off and let him out of his cage. I just say it as I see it. Most of the stuff that I have been forced to endure over summer has been so diabolical it's enough to turn me to read. Several shows have been so atrocious that I refused to write about them on principle, purely because I didn't want to give them any oxygen. Yep, that's me with the morals.

After a night of beautifully crafted piss-funny comedy, I felt as though I'd had a good feed, a long massage and a top root. The desolate ghost town that has been the past five weeks of programming probably helped intensify the impact. We're on stage-three water restrictions but the television drought is over! Allah be praised!

The new *Extras* is about 45 million times better than the last series and the last series of *Little Britain* is pure comedy gold and gets better with each watch.

Gervais actually does some proper actoring in this new season of *Extras*, but it doesn't really matter – I'd be happy for him to play David Brent for the rest of his life. Treats include Orlando Bloom playing a vain wanker, Daniel Radcliffe as a sex-starved wannabe and as for David Bowie, I laughed so much I lost a lung.

Gervais' stand-up DVDs are also surprisingly good, particularly *Politics*. That man has not just been hit with the funny stick; he's been rogered senseless by it. Gervais recently did a ripper interview with another comedy god, *Curb Your Enthusiasm*'s Larry David (co-creator of *Seinfeld*), and I caught a bit of it on YouTube. Well worth a squiz.

I'm not proud of it but I must admit that I wasn't crazy about the first series of *Extras*. Nor was I immediately in, hook, line and sinker, with *The Office* or *Little Britain*. Maybe I'm discerning, maybe I'm a little bit stupid. But after a few episodes I was writing their names on my exercise books with swirly writing in glitter pen.

Thank God for English comedy. Don't bother about saving the Queen but keep your filthy mitts off the BBC. I cut my teeth on *Monty Python*, *The Young Ones*, *The Fast Show* and *Big Train* and I love them all so much I want to kiss them on the mouth and touch them on the pants. And despite being so Captain Serious Pants, the British are bang up for a bit of breastfeeding adults, old ladies urinating and gratuitous swearing. It's so wrong, I love it.

The Bill

Am I the only person who wants to kill myself when I watch *The Bill*? Don't get me wrong, I think actors with rough heads should get work just as much as the next person, it's just that even the theme music conjures up the trifecta of sweaty Poms, bleak pubs and crims from the council estates who "never seen nuffink." As my eyes start to glaze over, I fish the remote control out from down the back of the couch; I flick three laps of the channels and occasionally find that it's the best thing on.

Sure, *The Bill*'s not as new and shiny as other whiz-bang fandangled programs. No fancy SMS-ing, no fancy stunts, no fancy basic dental hygiene. Just gritty, real-life cop drama with solid plot lines, consistent acting and more than its fair share of deep-fried food. Sometimes I can't help thinking that it's a little too gritty and real life. Would it kill them to have a pot plant? A blue sky? An attractive person? Sure *Cop Shop* was pretty bleak, but at least it had Paula Duncan with big hair, lip gloss and blue eye shadow and John Orcsik in his '70s sex-god glory; hairy chest, body shirts and all.

I thought I might need to explain *The Bill* until I remembered that everyone in the known world has seen at least one episode. There are even cannibals living in the most remote jungle in Africa only accessible by three-day trek, canoe and carrier pigeon that, when asked about *The Bill* will say "I lost interest when Polly went to prison and the station burned down."

Credit where credit's due, *The Bill* has successfully managed to reinvent itself for 20 years. But would it kill someone to crack a smile?

Sun Hill is England's Mount Thomas – a sleepy little suburb where there's a 76 per cent chance of being shot, bashed or winked at by a creepy old cop called Reg. Every episode is guaranteed to have at least one car chase ending in a dead-end cobbled alley with a pasty-faced cop slamming some poor git into a cyclone fence and saying "You're nicked."

It's never "Goody! Put on the answering machine and crack a bottle of red. *The Bill* is on!" It's more a case of "Well if it's a competition between having a conversation with the wife or watching *The Bill*, flick on and watch bobbies going the bonk."

The plodding feet in the credits are no longer, and Bernie from the Nolan Sisters has hung up her epaulettes and made a fitness DVD, but nothing much at Sun Hill has changed. There's a good two-parter starting 21 October revolving around a feud between two gangs, one called "The Skin

Man Massive," and featuring the line "You're nicked, you toe rag." It's not bad telly; it's just not great telly. If I want to be depressed I'd rather weigh myself, read my credit card bill or remember how good *Wildside* and *Janus* were.

Fat People on TV I

No media can do crap better than television. And I should know; I've been writing for TV for 14 years. When a program escalates from plain old sloppy work and contempt for the viewer's intelligence to award-winning, hand over the mouth, eyes like saucers, gasping desperately for air, you know that television has struck gold. Because you're not going to switch off now.

Then you throw fat people into the mix and you are talking triple-platinum, top-shelf, black-label shit. Imagine the meeting when it suddenly dawned on network execs that the ritual humiliation of fat people on television was surefire ratings gold. "Hang on, Gary, we can't have a fat chick reading the news. But there's no reason we can't have her suspended by a crane two inches above a wheelbarrow of chocolate eclairs."

"Ian, you're a genius."

"Next, the disabled, the mentally ill, pensioners."

"Hold your horses, Ian. Let's run out of fat people first."

After my typical weekend of rum, sodomy and the lash and chips, dips and nibbles, I love nothing more than popping on the hairshirt and flagellating myself to the tune of Nine's Sunday night hour of shame.

It starts at 6.30 with *Turn Back Your Body Clock*. Meet Dr Una. She is a slim, attractive, cool-headed shock-doc whose hobbies include inciting panic and reinforcing stereotypes and she is fluent in monosyllabic apocalyptic rhetoric. Then throw in a Big Fat Slob who hasn't exercised since petrol was under $1 a litre. Using the latest thermal imaging, she gives the BFS a predicted death age and then she and her mate the personal trainer torture the BFS. My favourite moment so far was when she said to this BFS: "You have a condition called gynecomastia. I'm not sure whether you are aware but it's essentially man boobs." I'm not a doctor but I am fairly certain that he was aware of his 16DD hooters. She then said: "Drinking hard makes you more of a woman than a man." Oooh, that hurt. But not as much as flicking his bra strap.

Next stop at 7 pm is *You Are What You Eat*. This is essentially the same show without the thermal imaging or the predicted death age. Presenter Gillian McKeith uses something else to shame and humiliate the BFS – their poo. That's right. Gillian has an alarming fascination with poo. She gets them to back one out and then discusses with them, at length, the stinkiness, stickiness and overall character of their offering and if it looks like a Picnic bar she tells them they are not chewing enough. Gillian doesn't mince words. Instead of saying something like, "So, Mandi, do you think that you may need some guidance with your issues surrounding food?" she'll be as likely to say "Hey Fatso! Lay off the pies."

These shows are the television equivalent of what they are telling us not to eat. As a great woman once said: "It's not that they are fat. It's not that they are stupid. It's not that they are prepared to be humiliated on television. It's that they are all three."

To be continued...

Fat People on TV II

Don't get me started about fat people on telly. Heavens to Betsy! I think you already have! Anyway, as I was saying last week, back to the Fat Freak Festival that has inveigled itself on to television where content used to be. Did you see *The Biggest Loser Engaged Couples* on Ten the other week? No? Well, you obviously have something that I don't. It's called a life. Let me fill you in on what you missed. Two couples went head to head for a $50,000 dream wedding (which will bookend perfectly with their $50,000 nightmare divorce.) After losing about 60 kilos per couple they were still ugly, stupid morons. But thinner. The winning couple was getting married in a castle. So she could be a princess. Here's a tip for you: it's all downhill from there, sweetheart. And you'll know you're at the bottom of that hill when you are hiding Mars bars in the glove box.

Ten may as well change its logo from *Seriously Ten* to *Seriously Fat* with its latest offering to the unwashed masses, *Honey, We're Killing the Kids*. Imagine people feeding their children crap all day, every day, for the kid's entire life. All with unlimited access to television. And a couch. Then imagine that these were real people from real life and that suddenly, for no apparent reason, the parents were so desperate for help they would allow themselves to be humiliated and shamed on national television. Well, imagine no more.

Are these shows helping to address the obesity epidemic? In a word, no. But gosh, it's fun pointing and laughing at the wobblers. So how can television help, apart from becoming pedal-powered? By producing more shows such as *It's A Fat, Fat World*, which SBS screened last Friday.

Here was a well-made, balanced and thorough look at the issues from a global perspective; the causes, the effects and the ultimate challenge before us. Don't worry about the bird flu, it's the cheese burgers that are going to get us. It is terrifying that in this day and age we have morbidly obese people who are actually undernourished because of their deadly addiction to food. And millions starving to death. But enough about the cast of *The OC*.

If you're after sensationalised titillation thinly veiled as human interest, Channel Nine's recent screening of *Eating Themselves to Death* takes the cake. (Don't excuse the pun, enjoy it.) Lucky viewers got to perv on and judge four morbidly obese people who weighed up to 318 kilos each, clothed in everything from bra and undies to totally naked apart from a pad between their legs. Dignity? You won't find it here. Look forward to more in this series of shock-docs from Nine, with titles that include (I kid you not) *Chubby Chasers*, *Amputee Admirers* and *The Smallest People In The World.*

How long will it be until we have an entire channel devoted solely to fat shows? Not soon enough, if you ask me. Chubby current affairs with *60 Inches*; morbidly obese gardening in *Backyard Bumcracks*; some drama with *McLeod's Drawstring Pants*; or *Law And Order (Fatty Boombah).* Let's not get into "adult movies"; before you know it I'll start talking about *Debbie Does Doughnuts.*

Fat People on TV III

Winter is perfect telly time. Summer telly is rubbish, autumn is still summer these days, and by spring we're over telly and trying to resuscitate our gardens and social lives. Winter is trackie daks, block of chockie, blankie over the knees and remote control in hand. We don't go out, not because it's nippy, but because we've put on 5 kilos and we can't fit into our jeans. And we'll watch anything. We'll watch things that under normal circumstances we wouldn't normally waste breath slagging off.

When people start waxing lyrical about *Coxy's Big Break*, *Antiques Roadshow* or *Quizmania*, you know that we have hit the depths of winter and the deepest, darkest pits of television.

Blame the cold if you will, or the fact that I can't fit into my jeans, but I have been sucked into *Teen Fit Camp*. Like winter food it's warm, a little on the heavy side and best served with hot butterscotch pudding, whipped cream and lashings of self-hatred.

Teen Fit Camp was called *Teen Fat Camp* until Network Ten decided to show some fake sensitivity to the fatties, wobblers and porkers. Not because the network has a social conscience, it just an attempt to delude viewers into thinking it does. Deep in its heart I'm sure the marketing department would have loved to call the show *Camp Lard Arse, Would You Like Fries with That?* or *Check Out the Tits on that 16-year-old Lad!*

I'm riveted. But, of course, I'm a little torn between "Is this exploitation?" or "Is this valuable social commentary?" But not torn enough to stop watching. Just torn enough to eat another chocolate biscuit. It's a battle and, all jokes aside, I can relate to them. Poor bastards.

Obese Aussie teens are sent off to camp in the American wilderness for eight weeks. They experience healthy living along with the odd pash, meltdown, epiphany and pigout-induced vomit. There are tears, triumphs, shocks, soul searching and broken hearts. It's not a "must-see," more a "might-see," but quite a decent show. So decent that it didn't thrive in its prime-time slot. And why would it? Seeing as though the makers chose not to employ any emotion-swelling music, before-and-after computerised graphics, intruders or fabricated tasks. It's a real documentary about a bunch of real kids going on a real journey. As opposed to the fake journeys we have become accustomed to.

Last year's ABC series *Brat Camp* was a similar idea, but instead of featuring teenagers on the chunky side of pudgy we're talking kids off the rails in a kind of drug, alcohol, death-wish kind of way. *Brat Camp: What Happened Next* checks up on the little scoundrels a year later. It's worth a look to see how these kids who were close to death, jail or life on the streets are faring now, even if you didn't see it the first time. But whatever you do, stay indoors and don't try on those jeans.

Iron Chef

You know you're in Asia when your kids want an icy pole and the only flavours available are red-bean paste or corn. And you know you're in Japan when you flick on the telly and find yourself watching contestants guessing which insect or reptile is walking over their head. Or a cartoon featuring a crack team of timid yet sexually adventurous female police-officers who fight crime in giant robot suits when they are not flat having group sex. *The Powder Puff Girls* meets, how can I put this, a gang of sluts.

I suppose none of this is surprising coming from a rich and dense culture with centuries of tradition and brilliant academics on one hand, and a dating agency called The Clap on the other.

I love *Iron Chef* because it combines my three greatest loves: food, all things Asian and taking the piss. *Iron Chef* is a masterpiece. It's the unlikely but successful fusion of cooking, medieval battle and Asian kitsch. Chairman Kaga? Words escape me. Think Priscilla Queen of the Kitchen, dressed by Liberace, lines from one of Russell Crowe's worst poems and acting more wooden than the horse in *Troy*. Most of the chairman's sentences start with, "If memory serves me correctly" and end with an evil grin, a theatrical flourish or a thoughtful look. All from a sequined man who loves a bit of cape and full-length glove action.

The challenger selects their iron chef. Chairman Kaga then excitedly announces that, "Today's theme ingredient is – fermented bean paste!" No wonder he's so thrilled.

The two then slog it out for an hour while a hyperventilating bloke called Ohta-san reports back to the commentators. He's kind of the Japanese Steve Jacobs (Nine's weatherman). He spends the "battle" breathlessly interjecting with "Fukui-san? Fukui-san? The challenger says that he is almost certain he won't finish his *foie gras* and smoked organ stew."

The tasters usually consist of a crusty old academic, a post-menopausal food critic and a young "actress." The actress is filmed in extreme close-up at various angles savouring her food as if she were performing the happy ending part of a massage. She also makes insightful comments such as "This is so good. Mmm. I like it a lot," and "This is so nice. I feel so happy to be eating it. Mmm. Yes."

The food critic says things like "Mmm. This rice is not

very Japanese. In Japan we prefer longer rice. No, this risotto is not so Japanese."

You can have your Nigella, your Jamie and your Stefano di Pieri. Give me a show that makes desserts using pork, sardines or, as in last Saturday's battle, sea cucumber. The food is not so much food that you eat as food that you would flush down the toilet.

The winner receives no trophy, medal or hand-set diamond-studded memento from Bruce and Walsh. Even guests on *World of Sport* used to at least get a bottle of Patra orange juice and half-a-dozen Four'n'Twenty pies. The winner of *Iron Chef* gets something money cannot buy: "The people's ovation and fame forever."

The Apprentice

The equation of reality television, highly competitive corporate maggots and Donald Trump equals morally bankrupt television void of all creativity and merit. That's right, *The Apprentice* is back. And like the previous four seasons, it would be of more benefit to spend the hour stabbing yourself in the eye with a safety pin.

Elimination shows such as *Big Brother*, *Survivor* and *The Biggest Loser* are the television equivalent of crack: truly evil, highly addictive and amazing value for money. I checked out the first few episodes, despite my concern that I could turn into one of those freaks who grab you at parties, fix your gaze and demand, "Are you watching *The Apprentice*?" And if you say "No" they look at you like you have just asked them to suck out the entire contents of your nose.

You can get an inkling of how shallow, repulsive and

repellent the "candidates" are when I tell you that Donald Trump was the person I warmed to most. If you've never seen the show, 18 greedy, two-faced, backstabbing, soulless corporate predators vie for the honour of becoming Donald Trump's bitch; sorry, I mean apprentice. Basically it's a competition to find the biggest arsehole. Tune in to watch the "candidates" suck up to Trump. You've never seen such grovelling and bare-faced brown-nosing. All it would take would be for Trump to say the word, and each and every one of them would drop their daks, brace themselves against his desk and assume the position.

"Good morning, Mr Trump!" "Certainly, Mr Trump!" "May I have the honour of cleaning your toe jam with my tongue, Mr Trump?" The only person I address as Mr is Mr Potato Head, who has better hair than Trump.

Trump's supermodel daughter Ivanka turns up in this series and at one stage says, "The bathrobes didn't speak to the quality of this brand," which is my second favourite quote from the show so far, after, "Second place is first in a long line of losers." Deep.

You get a real insight into this chicken-pecking experiment when you check out the candidates with their clear skin, sparkling eyes, gleaming teeth and model looks. Apart from one fat, pig-faced weasel with bad skin, too much product and a tie that screams halitosis. When they are asked to choose teams it comes as no surprise that after choosing "the gorgeous man in the orange tie" and "the beautiful girl in the brown," Pigface is referred to as "the man to the left" and chosen last. I hate good-looking, confident, smart people, so was immediately barracking for Pigface. Until it turned out that he is an ugly, loudmouthed twat who needs a good punch in the pants.

I'm hoping for an Australian version – brain-dead bogans being sent down to Bunnings to buy elbow grease, a left-handed spanner and a long weight. When they return empty-handed they're forced to form a naked human pyramid. That, I'd watch.

Medical Dramas

Doctor Mon is not just a legend because she used to do ward rounds with a Ventolin puffer in one hand and a packet of fags in the other. She's a legend because she's crap. I once asked her about a rash on my son's skin and she said "that's the badness coming out." She deals with kids and out of every 100 patients she tells 99 of the parents that the kid will grow out of it, and with the other one she shakes her head, sucks air through her teeth and asks them if they believe in God. To be fair, she does give them a choice of bad news or a spin of the wheel.

We recently spent a memorable evening dancing with taxi drivers, smoking hookahs and talking telly. (People at the Middle Eastern lounge will remember Dr Mon. She was the one who danced like she had electrodes attached to her genitals and asked if they had "A hookah with a heart of gold.")

So Dr Mon likes *ER*. And I don't know why, but I was surprised that a doctor would come home after a hard day of real-life drama to unwind with some fake real-life drama. I suppose it would be like me watching a show that was a fusion of *Prisoner*, *Honey We're Killing the Kids* and a documentary on retarded goats.

Dr Mon's love of medical dramas started with *The Young*

Doctors. Big hair, body shirts and pretty young things that lived on coffee scrolls and Passiona. Many of the doctors she knows love a bit of hospital drama too. But why? "Attractive people. Sex. Attractive people. More sex. All ends happily ever after even if they stuff up. There are no people who ask you questions you can't answer who then get pissed off and pull knives on you." And I thought she worked in a hospital, not Cash Converters.

She loves *Scrubs* (*ER* with jokes, if you ask me) and *Grey's Anatomy* (*Sex in the City* for doctors), but *House* is out because it's inaccurate and far-fetched. I adore *House*. Probably because I have a soft spot for social misfits, mavericks and any shows with lines such as "Union rules. I can't check out this guy's seeping gonorrhoea this close to lunch." Dr Mon reckons doctors would only tune into *Medical Emergency* or *RPA* if they were in it.

What about *Doctor Who*? "He's not a real doctor."

"How do you know?"

"No stethoscope."

According to my mole – and trust me, she is a mole – doctors are not immune to the fascination of shows such as *Amazing Medical Stories*. Just because they have spent half their life reading large books with tiny Latin writing doesn't mean they are any less interested in the deformed as other people. Like me.

As far as accuracy is concerned, it's hit and miss. But Dr Mon assures me the scene in *The Surgeon* where Sam Worthington was a doctor sucking on the nitrous oxide was alarmingly accurate. And common. But too common for Dr Mon. She prefers hookahs.

Amazing Medical Stories

I know I'm not a doctor although my credit card clearly says Dr Catherine Deveny. Long story, but due to the absence of a non-gender, status-free title such as "comrade" I was sick of telling people that, no, I was not a Mrs, a Miss or Ms, I was nothing. Only for conservative, narrow-minded, misogynist, uptight white honkies and inflexible computer systems assuming just because I had three children I must be a Mrs. Well, sucked in. I'm not even married.

The only people under the age of 50 who call themselves Mrs these days are vacant, spineless frumps who put currency on the notion of respectability in a misguided attempt to gain said non-existent and quite pedestrian attribute. The way I want to be remembered: as an irreverent maverick hoon. Dr Hoon to you.

Rebecca Harris thinks she's a doctor, but she's not a doctor. She's the host of *Amazing Medical Stories*: "On today's show the woman with cheetah legs, the little girl whose muscles are turning into bone, the boy who can't stop eating, a woman with a 70-kilo tumour that is crushing her to death and, after years as a circus novelty act, the man they call Woofboy just wants to fit in." Rename it *Wheel Out the Freaks*: *The Show That Dignity Forgot*.

You know when you hear the words "remarkable," "brave," "incredible," "extraordinary" and "fascinating" in one sentence we are talking exploitative voyeurism thinly veiled as human interest. I am a sucker for freaks, medical procedures and the extremities of human experience, so it keeps me watching. But that doesn't mean I feel good about it. Sure I watch, gasp and perv, but does that make it good television? I suppose that depends on your definition of good television and what you consider the point of television to be.

The story that I can't forget is the "remarkable journey" of a bright woman who had her extremely deformed legs amputated at a young age, a decision made by her fairly simple parents. She spends her life getting around on a skateboard and by climbing like a monkey. She grows up, falls in love and, miraculously, has a baby. Her mother dies a few months after the birth and so she moves back to the family home (which I would describe as a poky rundown shack) to care for her husband, son, father (who suffers dementia, schizophrenia and emphysema) and her intellectually disabled adult brother who has violent tendencies. And remember, she has NO LEGS. Amazing story, sure, but medical? What's in it for them to be filmed? A fridge full of cash, one hopes. But my guess is bugger all.

I am torn between the need to be open and raise awareness about disabilities and physical deformities and the concern that viewers are simply watching animals in a zoo. These people, who would have once only been able to survive as sideshow freaks, are still being treated as sideshow freaks. But it's OK because the show has the word "medical" in the title, so it has got to be good for you.

Top Gear

I drive a Volvo. Let's get that out in the open right now. So I am obviously no stranger to finding the humour in motoring. I love the Swedish brick and I'd take a bullet for my Volvo. My clapped-out jalopy has 410,000 kilometres on the clock, which makes it the auto equivalent of a 97-year-old man. If The Volvo's Rockin', Don't Bother Knockin', The Idle Needs Adjustin'.

Twice a year I call my mechanic and say "Hey, it's Catherine with the metallic phlegm-coloured Volvo that smells like cabbage. Can you drive it round the block, put a service sticker on it and charge me $200?" And he says, "Sure. Make it $150 'cause you look like a nice lady." You can have your fancy airbags and highfalutin indicators, just give me a car that handles like a three-bedroom house, looks like a coffin and guzzles so much fuel I have to put petrol on lay-by.

If you have never seen *Top Gear* you are in for a treat. I have been a fan of the show for almost as long as I have owned the above-mentioned car, which my hideous, ungrateful, spoilt kids refer to as "Mum's stinky old tractor."

Top Gear is a cult show about cars, now in its eighth series. Hosted by Jeremy Clarkson, James May and Richard Hammond, this British show is expertly made, extremely informative and hilarious. It's more than a television show. For diehard fans it's simply their reason to live.

It's the only motoring show on which you will hear lines like: "Listen to that engine. Sounds like Barry White eating wasps," or "Anyone who washes their car either has a small mind or an unhappy marriage," and "We're not going to listen to him because he's got a beard."

The presenters are passionate about cars and don't mince words. They are honest: "It's not so much a car as a shoe." Opinionated: "The only way you could possibly drive this car is with a box on your head, so no one could tell it's you." And scathing: "As something to live with every day, I would rather have bird flu."

Top Gear is famous for its stunts: having a nun drive a monster truck; dragging off helicopters in cars; people-mover racing; having teams of tiny Toyota Aygos play a game of soccer; and driving a Rolls-Royce into the local swimming pool for fun.

They once drove a Volvo 340 through a crusher while yelling, "This is for every time I've caught you dawdling at junctions, this is for every time I've caught you doing 4 miles per hour in a motorway. This is payback time!"

Unlike the usual car commercials and glossy brochures that are too up themselves and wanky for words, this show takes the piss and doesn't tip-toe around in fear of offending advertisers. Tune in to hear lines like, "You do not just avoid the Suzuki Wagon R. You avoid it like you would avoid unprotected sex with an Ethiopian transvestite."

You don't even need to own a car to enjoy this show – just a TV.

Australia's Best Backyards

I have three words for you, my friends: *Australia's Best Backyards*. You're going to assume that because this program is on Channel Seven, and because it's a bit suburban, I'm going to go in swinging, have a good spray, take the piss out of people who like garden gnomes and make a joke involving the word root.

Well guess what? I liked it. You didn't see that coming now did you? If I weren't such a loudmouth I'd be an enigma.

When I hear the term Great Australian Dream I can't help thinking of that dream where I'm at school without my pants on. It's high time that the Great Australian Dream was updated from a quarter-acre block and a roof to yell at your spouse under to: winning Tattslotto, paying off your HECS debt, telling your boss to get stuffed and waking up with the body of a 24-year-old (lying next to you).

Australia's Best Backyards is a good old stickybeak at Australia's best backyards. Now, when I use the term backyard we're talking: a breathtaking and massive English garden designed by Paul Bangay; a bush retreat featuring a man-made billabong, which doubles as a lap pool, a water catchment and a bush fire-fighting system; and a family house with a party backyard that would put a five-star resort in Bali to shame, complete with pools, outdoor cabana and wet bar.

We're not talking azaleas, pergolas and pot plants here. Thirty minutes of viewing this show and you'll take one look at your own backyard and want to kill yourself. You'll be so crushed by shame that you'll vow to stop wasting your Saturdays reading badly written, half-baked smug rantings like this column. And it all cuts together with links, tips and demonstrations by – deep sigh – Jamie Durie.

The only difference between a straight man and a gay man is Jamie Durie. Jamie Durie is not gay. But old green fingers is a red-hot spunk. Richard Stubbs has a good head for radio, Phillip Ruddock has a good heart for refrigeration and Jamie Durie has a good face for television.

This man is every mum's dream son, dream son-in-law and dream Mother's Day gift. Did I mention that he was once in the Gold Coast all-male dance and cabaret show *Manpower*? That's right, he used to get his gear off for hen's nights. And now he's signed a lucrative deal with Oprah to be the resident gardener.

Sure, this show suffers like all those "you wish" shows from its fair whack of the words "stunning," "breathtaking" and "in-spoy-ring," but it's a good watch presented by passionate people. And the best thing is it's a lifestyle show with no Catriona Rowntree in sight, but an earthy, curvy, warm, real-looking presenter called Fiona Bruyn who knows what she's on about.

Stuff the backyards, it's worth tuning in just to watch Jamie Durie handle his hairy succulents. If he's good enough for Oprah, he's good enough for me.